First World War

and Army of Occupation

War Diary

France, Belgium and Germany

9 DIVISION
Divisional Troops
53 Brigade Royal Field Artillery,
Divisional Ammunition Column
and Divisional Trench Mortar Batteries
7 May 1915 - 31 January 1919

WO95/1753

The Naval & Military Press Ltd
www.nmarchive.com
Published in association with The National Archives

Published by

The Naval & Military Press Ltd

Unit 10 Ridgewood Industrial Park,

Uckfield, East Sussex,

TN22 5QE England

Tel: +44 (0) 1825 749494

www.naval-military-press.com

www.nmarchive.com

Contents

Document type	Place/Title	Date From	Date To
Heading	1753/1.		
Heading	9th Division 53rd Bbe R.F.A. Sep 1915-Sep 1916.		
Heading	9th Division 53rd Brigade R.F.A. Vol I,II,III 10.5-31.8.15.		
Heading	Headquarters 53rd Brigade R.F.A. (9th Division) May 10 To August 1915.		
Heading	Confidential War Diary of 53rd Brigade R.F.A. From 10/5/15 To 31/7/15.		
War Diary	Bordon.	10/05/1915	10/05/1915
War Diary	Havre, France.	11/05/1915	12/05/1915
War Diary	Bilques.	13/05/1915	15/05/1915
War Diary	St Sylvestre.	16/05/1915	16/05/1915
War Diary	Lamenegatte.	17/05/1915	20/05/1915
War Diary	Boisgrenier	20/05/1915	08/06/1915
War Diary	Erquinghem.	08/06/1915	14/06/1915
War Diary	Molinghem.	15/06/1915	24/06/1915
War Diary	Haut Tieux.	25/06/1915	25/06/1915
War Diary	Letouret.	26/06/1915	30/06/1915
War Diary	Bde Hd. Qrs		
War Diary	Le Touret	15/07/1915	31/07/1915
War Diary	Le Touret.	01/08/1915	14/08/1915
War Diary	L'Ecleme.	14/08/1915	31/08/1915
Heading	Headquarters, 53rd Brigade, R.F.A. (9th Division) September 1915.		
War Diary	Annequin.	01/09/1915	25/09/1915
War Diary	Battle Round Loos Operation N.A Loos Attack On Foose N.8.	25/09/1915	30/09/1915
Heading	Headquarters 53rd Brigade R.F.A. (9th Division) October 1915.		
War Diary		01/10/1915	29/10/1915
Miscellaneous	The following Changes Took Place In The Personnel Of The Brigade Dining The Quarter August-October.		
Heading	9th Div 53rd Bde RFA. Bls: 7,8. Nov. Dec 15.		
Heading	Headquarters 53rd Brigade R.F.A. (9th Division) November. December 1915.		
War Diary	Batteries S & E Of Ypres Brigade H.Q Just W. Of Kroistraot At Forle Road.	03/11/1915	03/11/1915
War Diary	At Ypres.	19/12/1915	22/12/1915
Heading	9th Divisional Artillery 53rd Bde. R.F.A. January, 1916.		
War Diary		07/01/1916	31/01/1916
Heading	9th Divisional Artillery 53rd Bde. R.F.A. February, 1916.		
War Diary	Nieppe.	20/02/1916	20/02/1916
Heading	9th Divisional Artillery 53rd Bde. R.F.A. March, 1916.		
War Diary	At Nieppe.	00/03/1916	00/03/1916
Heading	9th Divisional Artillery 53rd Bde. R.F.A. April, 1916.		
War Diary	Nieppe.	00/04/1916	00/04/1916
Heading	9th Divisional Artillery 53rd Bde. R.F.A. June, 1916.		
War Diary		01/06/1916	14/06/1916

Heading	9th Divisional Artillery 53rd Bde. R.F.A. May, 1916.		
War Diary	Nieppe.	27/05/1916	27/05/1916
Heading	9th Div. XIII. Corps. Division Transferred To IV. Corps, First Army, 25.7.16. War Diary. Headquarters, 53rd Brigade, R.F.A. July 1916.		
War Diary		01/07/1916	30/07/1916
Heading	9th Divisional Artillery 53rd Bde. R.F.A. August, 1916.		
War Diary		01/08/1916	31/08/1916
Miscellaneous	R.A. 9th Divisional No. 35th Aug. 31st 1916.	31/08/1916	31/08/1916
Heading	9th. Divisional Artillery. 53rd Bde. R.F.A. September, 1916. Broken Up In September: 53rd Bde. H.Q. Became H.Q. 52nd Bde. Batteries Absorbed By 50th & 51st Bdes.		
Miscellaneous	Broken Up In September.		
War Diary		31/08/1916	11/09/1916
Heading	1753/2.		
Heading	9th Divisional 9th Divl Ammn Column May 1915-1919 Sep.		
Heading	9th Divisional 9th. D.A.C. May To Oct.15.		
Heading	Headquarters 9th Divisional Ammunition Column May To October 1915.		
Heading	Confidential War Diary of 9th Divisional Ammunition Column From 1st May 1915 To 31st October 1915. Volume 1.		
War Diary	Bordon.	07/05/1915	11/05/1915
War Diary	Southampton.	12/05/1915	12/05/1915
War Diary	Havre.	13/05/1915	14/05/1915
War Diary	Stomer.	15/05/1915	15/05/1915
War Diary	Tilques.	16/05/1915	16/05/1915
War Diary	Stuyver	17/05/1915	18/05/1915
War Diary	Meteren	19/05/1915	05/06/1915
War Diary	Habien Artors.	06/06/1915	25/06/1915
War Diary	Ecquedecques	05/06/1915	28/06/1915
War Diary	Le Vertannoy.	28/06/1915	28/06/1915
War Diary	Robecq.	29/06/1915	02/07/1915
War Diary	Riez Du Vinage.	02/07/1915	31/07/1915
War Diary	Riez.	29/07/1915	29/07/1915
War Diary	Riez Du Vinage.	01/08/1915	15/08/1915
War Diary	Cantrainne.	15/08/1915	02/09/1915
War Diary	Annezin.	02/09/1915	30/09/1915
War Diary	Annezin.	21/09/1915	29/09/1915
War Diary	Steenwerck	01/10/1915	01/10/1915
War Diary	Poperinghe.	02/10/1915	31/10/1915
Heading	9th Division Nov, Dec 1915.		
Heading	Headquarters 9th Divisional Ammunition Column November. December 1915.		
War Diary	Near Poperinghe.	01/12/1915	31/12/1915
War Diary	Near Poperinghe.	01/11/1915	30/11/1915
Heading	9th Divisional Artillery 9th Divisional Ammunition Column, January,1916.		
Heading	Confidential War Diary of 9th Divisional Ammunition Column From January 1st 1916 January 31st 1916. Volume. III.		
War Diary	Borre.	01/01/1916	31/01/1916
Heading	9th Divisional Artillery 9th Divisional Ammunition Column. February, 1916.		

Heading	Confidential War Diary of The 9th Divisional Ammunition Column R.F.A. From Feb 1st 1916 To Feb 29th 1916.		
War Diary	Borre.	01/02/1916	29/02/1916
Heading	9th Divisional Artillery 9th Divisional Ammunition Column, April, 1916.		
Heading	Confidential War Diary of The 9th Divisional Ammunition Column R.F.A. From April 1st 1916 To April 30th 1916. (Volume 6).		
War Diary	Schaexken.	01/04/1916	30/04/1916
War Diary	Schaexken.	13/04/1916	13/04/1916
Heading	9th Divisional Artillery 9th Divisional Ammunition Column, May, 1916.		
Heading	Confidential War Diary of The Ninth Divisional Column From May 1st 1916 To May 31st 1916. Volume.1.		
War Diary		01/05/1916	31/05/1916
Heading	9th Divisional Artillery 9th Divisional Ammunition Column, June, 1916.		
War Diary	Borre.	01/06/1916	01/06/1916
War Diary	Roquetoire.	01/06/1916	30/06/1916
Heading	9th Divisional Artillery 9th Divisional Ammunition Column, March, 1916.		
Heading	Confidential War Diary of 9th Divisional Ammunition Column R.F.A. From March 1st 1916 To March 31st 1916. Volume 5.		
War Diary	Borre.	01/03/1916	10/03/1916
War Diary	Schaexken.	11/03/1916	31/03/1916
Heading	9th Div. XIII. Corps. Division Transferred To IV. Corps, First Army, 25.7.16. War Diary. 9th Division Ammunition Column. July 1916.		
War Diary	Sailly-Le-Sec.	01/07/1916	07/07/1916
War Diary	Bois Des Tailles.	09/07/1916	17/07/1916
War Diary	Grovetown.	18/07/1916	20/07/1916
War Diary	Vaux Sur Somme.	28/07/1916	28/07/1916
War Diary	Allonville.	29/07/1916	29/07/1916
War Diary	Bouchon.	30/07/1916	30/07/1916
Heading	9th Divisional Artillery 9th Divisional Ammunition Column, August, 1916.		
War Diary	Longpre Pont Remy.	01/08/1916	01/08/1916
War Diary	Magnicourt.	01/08/1916	09/08/1916
War Diary	Houvelin.	10/08/1916	10/08/1916
War Diary	Houvelin And Division.	10/08/1916	12/08/1916
War Diary	Caucourt And Heripre.	13/08/1916	31/08/1916
Heading	9th Divisional Artillery 9th Divisional Ammunition Column, September, 1916.		
War Diary	Caucourt.	01/09/1916	30/09/1916
War Diary	Heripre.	01/09/1916	30/09/1916
Heading	9th Divisional Artillery 9th Divisional Ammunition Column, October, 1916.		
War Diary	Caucourt.	01/10/1916	05/10/1916
War Diary	Magnicourt.	05/10/1916	08/10/1916
War Diary	Rebreuviette.	09/10/1916	09/10/1916
War Diary	Groucnes.	10/10/1916	10/10/1916
War Diary	Villers Bocage.	11/10/1916	11/10/1916
War Diary	Behencourt.	11/10/1916	13/10/1916

War Diary	Becourt.	13/10/1916	31/10/1916
Heading	9th Divisional Artillery 9th Divisional Ammunition Column, November, 1916.		
War Diary	Becourt.	01/11/1916	17/11/1916
War Diary	Behencourt	24/11/1916	24/11/1916
War Diary	Talmas.	27/11/1916	27/11/1916
War Diary	Barly.	28/11/1916	28/11/1916
War Diary	Rebreuviette.	29/11/1916	30/11/1916
Heading	9th Divisional Artillery 9th Divisional Ammunition Column, December, 1916.		
War Diary	Rebreuviette.	01/12/1916	27/12/1916
War Diary	Wanquetin.	27/12/1916	31/01/1917
War Diary	Wanquetin.	15/01/1917	31/03/1917
War Diary	Wanquetin.	28/03/1917	28/03/1917
War Diary	Larisset.	01/04/1917	08/04/1917
War Diary	Maroeuil.	09/04/1917	09/04/1917
War Diary	Anzin.	10/04/1917	30/04/1917
War Diary	Anzin.	10/04/1917	03/05/1917
War Diary	Anzin.	18/05/1917	27/06/1917
War Diary	Agny Achicoort Beaurains.	01/07/1917	31/07/1917
War Diary	Agny.	01/08/1917	03/08/1917
War Diary	Lechelle.	03/08/1917	03/08/1917
War Diary	Equancourt.	08/08/1917	31/08/1917
War Diary	Equancourt.	27/08/1917	02/09/1917
War Diary	Behagnies.	03/09/1917	03/09/1917
War Diary	Watou.	07/09/1917	07/09/1917
War Diary	Vlamertinghe.	10/09/1917	12/09/1917
War Diary	Poperinghe.	15/09/1917	05/10/1917
War Diary	Hamhoek.	06/10/1917	06/10/1917
War Diary	Vlamertinghe.	09/10/1917	20/10/1917
War Diary	Poperinghe.	20/10/1917	20/10/1917
War Diary	Wormhoudt.	21/10/1917	21/10/1917
War Diary	Ghyvelde.	22/10/1917	22/10/1917
War Diary	Coxyde.	29/10/1917	20/11/1917
War Diary	Ghyvelde.	21/11/1917	21/11/1917
War Diary	Wormhoudt.	22/11/1917	22/11/1917
War Diary	Zermezeele.	23/11/1917	23/11/1917
War Diary	Bandringhem.	24/11/1917	24/11/1917
War Diary	Merck St. Lievin.	25/11/1917	25/11/1917
War Diary	Lespinoy.	26/11/1917	01/12/1917
War Diary	Doingt	02/12/1917	02/12/1917
War Diary	Marquaix.	03/12/1917	03/12/1917
War Diary	Bussu.	09/12/1917	17/12/1917
War Diary	Nurlu.	31/12/1917	28/02/1918
Heading	9th Div. War Diary. 9th Divisional Ammunition Column, R.F.A. March 1918.		
War Diary	Haut Allaines	01/03/1918	01/03/1918
War Diary	St. Radegonde.	04/03/1918	04/03/1918
War Diary	Moislains.	13/03/1918	27/03/1918
Heading	9th Divisional Artillery. 9th Divisional Ammunition Column R.F.A. April 1918.		
War Diary	Toutencourt.	01/04/1918	02/04/1918
War Diary	Locre.	03/04/1918	03/04/1918
War Diary	Westoutre.	11/04/1918	11/04/1918
War Diary	Poperinghe.	15/04/1918	13/05/1918
War Diary	Winnezeele.	13/05/1918	17/05/1918

War Diary	Racquinghem	17/05/1918	26/05/1918
War Diary	Eecke.	26/05/1918	30/06/1918
War Diary	Eecke.	17/06/1918	22/07/1918
War Diary	St. Sylvestre.	01/08/1918	01/08/1918
War Diary	Cappel.	30/08/1918	30/08/1918
War Diary	V.12.a. (Sheet: 27).	01/08/1918	23/08/1918
War Diary	Fletre (Near).	31/08/1918	31/08/1918
War Diary	Wardrecques Area.	24/08/1918	31/08/1918
War Diary	St Sylvestre Cappel.	31/08/1918	31/08/1918
War Diary	Caestre (Near).	01/09/1918	12/09/1918
War Diary	Haandekat Area.	12/09/1918	27/09/1918
War Diary	Hamhoek Area	27/09/1918	28/09/1918
War Diary	Vlamertinghe.	28/09/1918	28/09/1918
War Diary	Ypres.	29/09/1918	30/09/1918
War Diary	Potijze.	01/10/1918	14/10/1918
War Diary	Keiberg Slypscappel.	14/10/1918	14/10/1918
War Diary	Rolleghem Cappelle	15/10/1918	20/10/1918
War Diary	Rolleghem Cappelle	17/10/1918	17/10/1918
War Diary	St. Catherine Cappell	20/10/1918	22/10/1918
War Diary	Stokerij.	22/10/1918	25/10/1918
War Diary	Harlebeke.	25/10/1918	31/10/1918
War Diary	Huele.	01/11/1918	13/11/1918
War Diary	Vichte.	14/11/1918	14/11/1918
War Diary	Renaix.	15/11/1918	15/11/1918
War Diary	Nederbrakel.	18/11/1918	18/11/1918
War Diary	Tenbosch.	20/11/1918	20/11/1918
War Diary	Neyghem	21/11/1918	21/11/1918
War Diary	Tourneppe	23/11/1918	23/11/1918
War Diary	Bierges.	25/11/1918	25/11/1918
War Diary	Huppaye.	27/11/1918	27/11/1918
War Diary	Moxhe.	28/11/1918	28/11/1918
War Diary	Ampsin.	29/11/1918	29/11/1918
War Diary	Vaux-Sur Chevremont.	01/12/1918	04/12/1918
War Diary	Verviers.	04/12/1918	04/12/1918
War Diary	Eupen.	05/12/1918	05/12/1918
War Diary	Merode.	06/12/1918	06/12/1918
War Diary	Kerpen.	07/12/1918	07/12/1918
War Diary	Bocklemund.	08/12/1918	08/12/1918
War Diary	Stammheim.	13/12/1918	13/12/1918
War Diary	Langenfeld.	15/12/1918	15/12/1918
War Diary	Ohligs.	21/12/1918	31/05/1919
War Diary	Ohligs. Germany	01/06/1919	01/08/1919
War Diary	Kirchtroisdorf.	01/08/1919	01/09/1919
War Diary	Elsdorf.	29/09/1919	29/09/1919
Heading	1753/3.		
Heading	9th Division 9th Divl Trench Mortar Btts. Jly 1916-1919 Jan.		
Heading	9th Divisional Artillery 9th Divl. Trench Mortar Batteries. July, 1916.		
Miscellaneous	Head Quarters. 9th Division.	02/09/1916	02/09/1916
War Diary	Somme.	01/07/1916	13/07/1916
War Diary	Longueval.	14/07/1916	31/07/1916
Heading	9th Divisional Artillery. 27th Trench Mortar Battery, July, 1916.		
War Diary	Billon Valley.	01/07/1916	02/07/1916
War Diary	Montauban.	03/07/1916	03/07/1916

War Diary	Montauban & Bernafay Wood.	04/07/1916	07/07/1916
War Diary	Billon Valley.	08/07/1916	13/07/1916
War Diary	Longueval.	13/07/1916	19/07/1916
War Diary	Talus Boise	20/07/1916	20/07/1916
War Diary	Citadel.	20/07/1916	22/07/1916
War Diary	Mericourt L'Abee.	23/07/1916	23/07/1916
War Diary	Hangest.	24/07/1916	24/07/1916
War Diary	Bellancourt.	25/07/1916	25/07/1916
War Diary	Brvay.	26/07/1916	30/07/1916
War Diary	Dieval	31/07/1916	31/07/1916
War Diary	Billon Valley.	01/07/1916	02/07/1916
War Diary	Montauban.	03/07/1916	04/07/1916
War Diary	Montauban & Bernafay Wood.	04/07/1916	07/07/1916
War Diary	Billon Valley.	08/07/1916	13/07/1916
War Diary	Longueval.	13/07/1916	19/07/1916
War Diary	Talus Boise	20/07/1916	20/07/1916
War Diary	Citadel.	21/07/1916	22/07/1916
War Diary	Mericourt L'Abee.	23/07/1916	23/07/1916
War Diary	Hangest.	24/07/1916	24/07/1916
War Diary	Bellancourt.	25/07/1916	25/07/1916
War Diary	Brvay.	26/07/1916	30/07/1916
War Diary	Dieval	31/07/1916	31/07/1916
Heading	9th Divisional Artillery. 27th Trench Mortar Battery, August, 1916.		
War Diary	Dieval	01/08/1916	12/08/1916
War Diary	Villers Aux Bois.	13/08/1916	24/08/1916
War Diary	(Careney Sector Trenchs).	25/08/1916	31/08/1916
Heading	9th Divisional Artillery 26th Trench Mortar Battery, August, 1916.		
Miscellaneous	Abject War Diaries To 37th Division Q.	12/09/1916	12/09/1916
War Diary		01/08/1916	31/08/1916
Heading	9th Divisional Artillery 9th Divl. Trench Mortar Batteries, August, 1916		
Miscellaneous	Officer i/c A.G's Office., Base.	08/09/1916	08/09/1916
Miscellaneous	9th DA./Herewith War Diary of this unit for the smith of August	09/09/1916	09/09/1916
War Diary	Monuival.	01/08/1916	14/08/1916
War Diary	Camblain.	15/08/1916	15/08/1916
War Diary	Vimy Ridge.	16/08/1916	31/08/1916
War Diary	In the field	01/08/1916	18/08/1916
War Diary	Villers au Bois	01/08/1916	20/08/1916
War Diary	Villers au Bois	16/08/1916	29/08/1916
War Diary	Villers au Bois	27/08/1916	31/08/1916
Heading	9th Divisional Artillery. 9th Divl. Trench Mortar Batteries, September, 1916.		
War Diary	Vimy Ridge.	01/09/1916	30/09/1916
Heading	9th Divisional Artillery. 9th Divisional Trench Mortar Batteries, October, 1916.		
War Diary	Vimy.	01/10/1916	10/10/1916
War Diary	Le Sars Line.	11/10/1916	31/10/1916
Heading	9th Divisional Artillery. 9th Divl. Trench Mortar Batteries, November, 1916.		
War Diary	Mametz Wood.	01/11/1916	13/11/1916
War Diary	St. Gratien.	14/11/1916	26/11/1916
War Diary	Mirvaux.	27/11/1916	29/11/1916
War Diary	Canettemont.	30/11/1916	30/11/1916

Heading	9th Divisional Artillery. 9th Divl. Trench Mortar Batteries. December, 1916.		
War Diary	Canettemont.	01/12/1916	26/12/1916
War Diary	Arras.	27/12/1916	31/12/1916
Miscellaneous	Brigade Major Riding.	03/02/1917	03/02/1917
War Diary	Arras.	01/01/1917	30/04/1917
Map			
War Diary	Arras.	01/05/1917	24/05/1917
War Diary	Anzin. St. Aubin.	25/05/1917	14/06/1917
War Diary	Foufflin Ricametz.	15/06/1917	26/06/1917
War Diary	Arras.	27/06/1917	27/06/1917
War Diary	Achicourt.	28/06/1917	05/07/1917
War Diary	Wanquetin.	06/07/1917	03/08/1917
War Diary	Vallartwood.	04/08/1917	07/08/1917
War Diary	Havrincourt Wood	08/08/1917	01/09/1917
War Diary	Ruyaulcourt.	02/09/1917	03/09/1917
War Diary	Sapignies.	04/09/1917	08/09/1917
War Diary	Near Watou.	09/09/1917	29/09/1917
War Diary	Near Poperinghe.	30/09/1917	06/10/1917
War Diary	Ham Hoek.	07/10/1917	22/10/1917
War Diary	Ghyvelde Area.	23/10/1917	29/10/1917
War Diary	Coxyde Bains.	30/10/1917	22/11/1917
War Diary	Beaurainville.	23/11/1917	01/12/1917
War Diary	Doingt	02/12/1917	07/12/1917
War Diary	Heudicourt.	08/12/1917	31/01/1918
War Diary	Marley Camp.	14/02/1918	28/02/1918
War Diary	Heudicourt.	01/02/1918	04/02/1918
War Diary	Marley Camp.	05/02/1918	13/02/1918
Heading	9th Div. 9th Div. Trench Mortar Brigade. March 1918.		
War Diary	Marley Camp Near Bray.	01/03/1918	01/03/1918
War Diary	Haut Allaines.	02/03/1918	04/03/1918
War Diary	Near Peronnes.	05/03/1918	11/03/1918
War Diary	Heudicourt.	12/03/1918	31/03/1918
Heading	9th Divisional Artillery. 9th Divisional Trench Mortar Brigade April 1918.		
War Diary	Teutencourt.	01/04/1918	03/04/1918
War Diary	Near Kemmel.	04/04/1918	15/04/1918
War Diary	Aragon Camp.	16/04/1918	19/04/1918
War Diary	Near Poperinghe.	20/04/1918	30/04/1918
War Diary	Camp Near Poperinghe	01/05/1918	16/05/1918
War Diary	Camp Near Racquinghen.	17/05/1918	25/05/1918
War Diary	Thieushouk.	26/05/1918	31/05/1918
War Diary	Near Thieushouk.	01/06/1918	02/06/1918
War Diary	Near Caestre.	03/06/1918	30/06/1918
War Diary	Near Caestre Q33d 75. 90 Sheet 27 S.E.	01/07/1918	31/07/1918
War Diary	Near Caestre Q.33d. 75.90 Sheet 27 S.E.	26/07/1918	12/09/1918
War Diary	Near Houtkerque.	13/09/1918	27/09/1918
War Diary	Ypres.	28/09/1918	30/09/1918
War Diary	Potijze.	01/10/1918	03/10/1918
War Diary	Keyberg.	04/10/1918	05/10/1918
War Diary	Ledeghem.	06/10/1918	15/10/1918
War Diary	Winkel St Eloi.	15/10/1918	21/10/1918
War Diary	Hulste.	21/10/1918	25/10/1918
War Diary	Beveren.	25/10/1918	29/10/1918
War Diary	Cuerne.	30/10/1918	30/11/1918
War Diary	Ampsin Belgium.	01/12/1918	31/12/1918

War Diary Lohdorf Near Ohligs. Germany. 01/01/1919 31/01/1919

9TH DIVISION

53RD BDE R.F.A.

SEP 1915 - SEP 1916.

Broken up Sep 1916

53 BDE RFA REFORMED 17 3 18
IN EGYPT 3 LAHORE DIVISION

9th Division

121/6242

53rd Brigade R. F. A.

Vols I, II, III.

10. 5 - ~~31. 7. 15~~

31. 8. 15

HEADQUARTERS

53rd BRIGADE R. F. A.

(9th Division)

MAY 10 to ~~XXXXX~~ AUGUST

1915

CONFIDENTIAL

WAR DIARY

of

53rd Brigade

R.F.A.

From 10/5/15 to 31/7/15

9th Div

Instructions regarding War Diaries and Intelligence Summaries are contained in F. S. Regs., Part II. and the Staff Manual respectively. Title pages will be prepared in manuscript.

WAR DIARY
or
INTELLIGENCE SUMMARY.
(Erase heading not required.)

Army Form C. 2118.

53rd Bde R.F.A
MAY 1915

Hour, Date, Place	Summary of Events and Information	Remarks and references to Appendices
1915 May		
10th BORDON	Left by troop train and embarked at SOUTHAMPTON for FRANCE	
11th HAVRE, FRANCE	disembarked and proceeded to standing camp No 1.	
12th " "	Entrained and proceeded by rail via ROUEN & BOULOGNE	
13th BILQUES	Reached WIZERNES station at 9.30 am and detrained. Proceeded to billets at BILQUES by route march distance 5 miles.	
14th & 15th "	Remained at BILQUES	
16th St SYLVESTRE	Marched to CASSEL district & billeted for night at St SYLVESTRE.	
17th LAMENEGATTE	Marched via METERAN and BAILLEUL to LAMENEGATTE near NIEPPE and went into billets there.	
18th do	A and B batteries moved up into action with 12th Bde RFA group S. of ARMENTIERES. and were attached to III corps VI division	
19th & 20th do	A and B fired at German lines to register their position and on night of 20th C and D batteries moved into action with 12th Bde RFA	
20th BOIS GRENIER	group. The B.A.C. remained at LAMENEGATTE	
21st to 24th "	A, B and D batteries were in action firing for registration. A battery taking part in small action against German post on night of 24th. C Battery engaged in preparing position.	
25th "	B battery moved into back billets out of action owing to hostile fire (Arch cannot be controlled.)	

(73989) W4141—463. 400,000. 9/14. H.&J.Ltd. Forms/C. 2118/10.

Instructions regarding War Diaries and Intelligence Summaries are contained in F. S. Regs., Part II. and the Staff Manual respectively. Title pages will be prepared in manuscript.

Army Form C. 2118.

WAR DIARY
or
INTELLIGENCE SUMMARY.
(Erase heading not required.)

Hour, Date, Place	Summary of Events and Information	Remarks and references to Appendices
1915 – May. 26th – BOIS GRENIER	Hd. Qrs of brigade moved forward & relieved the 12th N.M. R.F.A. HdQrs & took over charge of 12th Rd Group.	
" 25th – 31st "	A C and D batteries fired daily on enemy's position.	
	[illegible] Lt Colonel Comdg 53rd N.M. R.F.A.	

(73989) W4141—463. 400,000. 9/14. H.&J.Ltd. Forms/C. 2118/10.

Instructions regarding War Diaries and Intelligence Summaries are contained in F. S. Regs., Part II. and the Staff Manual respectively. Title pages will be prepared in manuscript.

WAR DIARY
or
INTELLIGENCE SUMMARY.
(Erase heading not required.)

Army Form C. 2118.

Hour, Date, Place	Summary of Events and Information	Remarks and references to Appendices
1915 June 1st BOIS GRENIER	B battery moved forward into action and occupied a new position	
" 1st to 6th – –	All batteries engaged – firing at former positions daily.	
" 7th–8th – –	All batteries withdrawn from forward positions on relief by batteries of 27th Div. One section being relieved each night and moving back to ERQUINGHEM. Bde HdQrs remained in charge of the area under 27th Div.	
" 8th to 14th ERQUINGHEM	Batteries in billets at ERQUINGHEM. Bde H.Qr at BOIS GRENIER	
" 14th –	A battery and 1 subsec of B.A.C transferred to 27th Div, and struck off the strength of the brigade. On the night of the 14th the brigade HdQrs and B, C, D batteries and B.A.C marched via LAGORGUE to MOLINGHAM to rejoin 9th division & went into billets there.	
" 15th to 24th MOLINGHEM	Remained at MOLINGHEM resting	
" 25th HAUT RIEUX	Marched to HAUT RIEUX en route to the front – billeted there	
" 26th LE TOURET	HQrs and B & C batteries marched to LE TOURET and occupied positions behind the RUE de BOIS.	
" 27th –	D battery and B.A.C. moved into forward position D battery behind RUE L'EPINETTE and B.A.C near ESSARS	
" 26th to 30th "	Batteries in action firing to register enemy's front.	

[illegible] Lt Colonel
Comg 52nd Bde RFA.

(73989) W4141—463. 400,000. 9/14. H.&J.Ltd. Forms/C. 2118/10.

53rd Brigade R. F. A.

Instructions regarding War Diaries and Intelligence Summaries are contained in F. S. Regs., Part II. and the Staff Manual respectively. Title pages will be prepared in manuscript.

WAR DIARY
or
INTELLIGENCE SUMMARY.
(*Erase heading not required.*)

Army Form C. 2118.

Hour, Date, Place	Summary of Events and Information	Remarks and references to Appendices
	Nominal roll of Officers with the Brigade when proceeding on active service	
Bde H^d Qrs	O.C. Bde . Lt Colonel K.K. Knapp.	
	Adjutant . Lieut (Temp) E.G. Reidy Transferred on 26.6.15	
	" Capt. K.H. Devitt appointed adjutant 26.6.15	from O.C. B.A.C.
	Orderly Offr. 2nd Lieut. C.H. Brittan	
	Medical Offr. Lieut. C.A. Smallhorn (attached). R.A.M.C.	
	Veterinary Offr. " Torrance A.V.C attached joined	
	Batteries & B.A. Column	

A Battery.	B Battery	C Battery	D Battery
Major D.C. Spencer Smith	Capt (Temp) A.J. Usborne	Major D. Reynolds V.C.	Major Hon H.R. Scarlett
Captain S.J. Pusanelli	2 Lieut F.B.B. Spragge	Temp 2 Lieut H.H. Macrostie	2 Lieut (Temp) T. Steven
Temp 2 Lieut D.N. Hossie	Temp 2 Lieut. L.H. Jacobson	" " D.E. Logan	" " F.M. Holman
Lieut M. Trowton	" " H.W.G. Duthy	" " A.N. King	" " W.S.B Parry.

Bde Ammn Column

Capt. K.H. Devitt appointed adjutant 26.6.15.
2 Lieut (Temp) W.A. Houston
2 Lieut " J.M.G. Bell

(73989) W4141—463. 400,000. 9/14. H.&J.Ltd. Forms/C. 2118/10.

Instructions regarding War Diaries and Intelligence Summaries are contained in F. S. Regs., Part II. and the Staff Manual respectively. Title pages will be prepared in manuscript.

Army Form C. 2118.

WAR DIARY
or
INTELLIGENCE SUMMARY.
(Erase heading not required.)

Hour, Date, Place	Summary of Events and Information	Remarks and references to Appendices
1915 JULY LE TOURET 1st to 31st	Nothing of special note. Batteries fire daily on portion of enemy's front line in reply to hostile fire. Situation unaltered throughout the month. [illegible] Lt Colonel Commdg 53rd Bde R.F.A.	

(73989) W4141—463. 400,000. 9/14. H.&J.Ltd. Forms/C. 2118/10.

IXth Div

Aug — Oct 1915 WB.iv, v, vi. 53rd Bde. R.F.A.

Instructions regarding War Diaries and Intelligence Summaries are contained in F. S. Regs., Part II. and the Staff Manual respectively. Title pages will be prepared in manuscript.

WAR DIARY
or
INTELLIGENCE SUMMARY.
(*Erase heading not required.*)

Army Form C. 2118.

Hour, Date, Place	Summary of Events and Information	Remarks and references to Appendices
1915 August 1 – 14 LE TOURET.	Nothing to report. Retaliation for hostile fire on our trenches carried out - otherwise very little shelling	
14th	The Brigade moved back to rest at L'ECLÈME being relieved by 37th Brigade.	
14 — 31 L'ECLÈME	Resting.	
31st	B/53 went up into action near CAMBRIN	
	[signature] Lt Colonel Comdg 53rd Bde RFA	

(73989) W4141—463. 400,000. 9/14. H.&J.Ltd. Forms/C. 2118/10.

WAR DIARY

Headquarters,

53rd BRIGADE, R.F.A.

(9th Division)

S E P T E M B E R

1 9 1 5

Sept 1915

Instructions regarding War Diaries and Intelligence Summaries are contained in F. S. Regs., Part II. and the Staff Manual respectively. Title pages will be prepared in manuscript.

WAR DIARY
or
INTELLIGENCE SUMMARY.
(Erase heading not required.)

Army Form C. 2118.

53rd Bde. R.F.A

Hour, Date, Place	Summary of Events and Information	Remarks and references to Appendices
September		
1st	D/53 went into action E of ANNEQUIN	
ANNEQUIN	Brigade H.Q. moved to ANNEQUIN	
2nd	C/53 went into action at TOURBIERES	
	In C/53 a Lyddite shell detonated just on leaving the gun - killing 4 & wounding 2 of the detachment.	
	The position of C/53 was located & shelled, one gun being damaged. The battery moved to a position just in front of ANNEQUIN.	
2nd to 20th	Batteries busy registering enemy's 2nd line trenches, communication trenches & points on first line; mostly with aeroplane observation. Gun pits made as far as possible shell-proof with double roof & air-space in between.	
21 to 24	Preliminary Bombardment ~~[illegible]~~ for attack on GERMAN position S of LA BASSÉE Road. No firing by the brigade during the day. Night firing started 6 p.m. ended 4 a.m. Each battery had two tasks each night & 120 rounds for each task.	

Instructions regarding War Diaries and Intelligence Summaries are contained in F. S. Regs., Part II. and the Staff Manual respectively. Title pages will be prepared in manuscript.

WAR DIARY

or

~~INTELLIGENCE SUMMARY.~~

(*Erase heading not required.*)

Army Form C. 2118.

Hour, Date, Place	Summary of Events and Information	Remarks and references to Appendices
ANNEQUIN. September 25. Battle round LOOS. Operations N. of LOOS. attack on FOSSE No 8.	The bombardment prior to assault began at 5.50 am. The Brigade was employed to form a barrage at the enemy's second line of defence. Barrage ceased at 7.25 am.	
1.0 pm	D/53 received orders to move forward in close support of 26th & 27th Infantry Brigades in an attack on HAISNES Village. The move was subsequently postponed & not carried out till 4 pm. Position occupied W. of HOHENZOLLERN Redoubt	HOHENZOLLERN Redoubt
	During the night D/53 withdrew to its original pits.	
September 26 & 27	The Brigade fired on strong points in & behind the enemy's front line which had not fallen. Fire kept up all night.	
28.	Fire as on previous day continued at intervals. No night firing.	

(73989) W4141—463. 400,000. 9/14. H.&J.Ltd. Forms/C. 2118/10.

Instructions regarding War Diaries and Intelligence Summaries are contained in F. S. Regs., Part II. and the Staff Manual respectively. Title pages will be prepared in manuscript.

WAR DIARY
or
INTELLIGENCE SUMMARY.
(Erase heading not required.)

Army Form C. 2118.

Hour, Date, Place	Summary of Events and Information	Remarks and references to Appendices
September 29		
9.25 am	Fired on hostile troops said to be collecting among houses for a counter attack. Fire reported successful in dispersing enemy.	
Sept 30	One section of each battery withdrawn & replaced by sections of batteries of 130 Bde. Guns & vehicles in the pits were left for incoming batteries; their guns being taken in exchange.	

[illegible] Lt Colonel
Comdg [illegible] Bde RFA

HAEDQUARTERS

x 53rd BRIGADE R. F. A.

(9th Division)

OCTOBER

1915

Army Form C. 2118.

WAR DIARY
or
INTELLIGENCE SUMMARY.
(Erase heading not required.)

*Instructions regarding War Diaries and Intelligence Summaries are contained in F. S. Regs., Part II. and the Staff Manual respectively. Title pages will be prepared in manuscript.

October 1915

53rd Brigade, R.F.A.

Place	Date	Hour	Summary of Events and Information	Remarks and references to Appendices
	October 1		The sections relieved marched to billets at STEENVOORDE	
		12 noon	O.C. 130 Bde. took over command from 53rd Brigade.	
			Remaining sections of 53rd Brigade withdrawn at dusk.	

(73989) W4141—463. 400,000. 9/14. H.&J.Ltd. Forms/C. 2118

T2134. Wt. W708—776. 500000. 4/15. Sir J. C. & S.

Instructions regarding War Diaries and Intelligence Summaries are contained in F. S. Regs., Part II. and the Staff Manual respectively. Title pages will be prepared in manuscript.

WAR DIARY
or
INTELLIGENCE SUMMARY.
(Erase heading not required.)

Army Form C. 2118.

Hour, Date, Place	Summary of Events and Information	Remarks and references to Appendices
October 2	Leading sections of batteries continued march to neighbourhood of YPRES. B/53 went into action S.E. of the town.	
October 3	Remaining sections formed up. C/53 + D/53 went into action at DICKEBUSCH ~~[illegible]~~ in positions vacated by 81st Brigade. 53rd Brigade H.Q. at DICKEBUSCH. All batteries placed under other brigades for tactical purposes.	
October 25th	The Regrouping of batteries of 53rd brigade (howitzer) B/53 under 50th Brigade, C/53 under 52nd brigade, D/53 under 51st brigade made a semi-permanent for tactical purposes, and D/50 D/51 D/52 batteries (18 Pr) placed under O.C. 53rd brigade for tactical purposes, the brigade becoming 4th [illegible] 9th Division artillery for tactical purposes. D/50 and D/52 were in action S. & S.E. of YPRES covering front from YPRES–COMINES Railway to a point in German front opposite our trench 47. D/51 [illegible]	

(73989) W4141—463. 400,000. 9/14. H.&J.Ltd. Forms/C. 2118/10.

Instructions regarding War Diaries and Intelligence Summaries are contained in F. S. Regs., Part II. and the Staff Manual respectively. Title pages will be prepared in manuscript.

WAR DIARY
or
INTELLIGENCE SUMMARY.
(*Erase heading not required.*)

Army Form C. 2118.

Hour, Date, Place	Summary of Events and Information	Remarks and references to Appendices
October 25th to — 28th & 29th	Usual fire in retaliation for hostile fire D/51 went into action S.E. of YPRES — relief of D/52 which moved to rest.	
	[illegible] Commdg 52nd Brigade R.F.A.	

Instructions regarding War Diaries and Intelligence Summaries are contained in F. S. Regs., Part II. and the Staff Manual respectively. Title pages will be prepared in manuscript.

WAR DIARY
or
INTELLIGENCE SUMMARY.
(*Erase heading not required.*)

Army Form C. 2118.

Hour, Date, Place	Summary of Events and Information	Remarks and references to Appendices
	The following changes took place in the personnel of the Brigade during the Quarter AUGUST - OCTOBER	
2/Lt G. B. Ellis, R.F.A.	Posted to B.A.C. 1-8-15	
Lt C.N. Smallhorn, RAMC	Transferred from attached to Hd Qtrs 53rd Bde to 9th Pioneer Battn,	1-8-15
Lt W.A. Troup, RAMC	" " 9th Pioneer Battn to Hd Qtrs 53rd Bde	R.F.A., 1-8-15.
" L.H. Torrance, A.V.C.	" attached to Hd Qtrs 53rd Bde to Vety Mobile	Section, 9th Division 1-9-15
" H. McCullough, A.V.C.	Attached to Hd Qtrs 53rd Bde from Vety Mobile Section 1-9-15 -	admitted Hospital &
Capt Doyle, A.V.C.	struck off strength 25-9-15	
"	Attached to Hd Qtrs 53rd Bde. 1-10-15	
Capt K.H. Dewitt, R.F.A.	Posted from Adjt 53rd Bde to 9th Divl Ammn Column 23-8-15.	
Lt. F. B. B. Spragge, R.F.A.	Appointed Adjt 53rd Bde, R.F.A., from B/53 - 23-8-15.	
2/Lt J.B.B. Spragge R.F.A.	} Promoted to Lieutenants 9-6-15	
2/Lt C.H. Brittan, R.F.A.	}	
2/Lt P.M. Holman, R.F.A.	Evacuated sick & struck off strength 18-8-15	
2/Lt H.A. Russell, R.F.A.	Posted to D/53 29-8-15	
do G.H. Smith R.F.A.	" " Bac 28-8-15 and transferred to B/53	23-8-15
do E.J. Gillett R.F.A.	Attached. 53rd Bde H.Q. 16-9-15 - severely wounded	& died of wounds 28 9/15.
do J.A. Atwell R.F.A.	Attached to 53rd Bde, R.F.A. 14-9-15	
do R.A. Nicolls R.F.A.	do " 4-9-15	
do H.H. Macroatie - C/53]	Promoted to Lieutenants on (date unknown at present	
do T. Stevens - D/53]		

(73989) W4141-463. 400,000. 9/14. H.&J.Ltd. Forms/C. 2118/10.

9th [illegible]

53rd Bde: RFA.

Vols: 7, 8.

121/7931

Nov Dec

15

[illegible]

HEADQUARTERS

53rd BRIGADE R. F. A.

(9th Division)

NOVEMBER .... DECEMBER

1915

Instructions regarding War Diaries and Intelligence Summaries are contained in F. S. Regs., Part II. and the Staff Manual respectively. Title pages will be prepared in manuscript.

WAR DIARY
or
INTELLIGENCE SUMMARY.
(Erase heading not required.)

Army Form C. 2118.

53rd Div Arty

Hour, Date, Place	Summary of Events and Information	Remarks and references to Appendices
November 3 Batteries S + E of YPRES Brigade HQ just W. of KRUISTRAAT at fork roads	D/52 went up into action 4th group employed to bring extra fire on any part of the Divisional front, one battery being registered on the whole front of each Infantry Brigade. D/50 in action at TROIS ROIS covering trenches of centre Infantry Brigade (D/51 in action between YPRES - MENIN Road & ROULERS Railway just E of L'ECOLE de BIENFAISANCE, covering the front of the right Infantry Brigade (D/52 close to D/51 covering the front of left Infantry Brigade (Only retaliatory fire & minor artillery enterprises during the month A. T. Belcher Lieut Col RFA Comdg 4th Group	

(73989) W4141—463. 400,000. 9/14. H.&J.Ltd. Forms/C. 2118/10.

Army Form C. 2118.

Instructions regarding War Diaries and Intelligence Summaries are contained in F. S. Regs., Part II. and the Staff Manual respectively. Title pages will be prepared in manuscript.

WAR DIARY
or
INTELLIGENCE SUMMARY.
(*Erase heading not required.*)

Hour, Date, Place	Summary of Events and Information	Remarks and references to Appendices
December		
at YPRES		
19 – 22	Relief of 9th D.A. in action by batteries of 50th D.A.	
	D/50 relieved by a battery of 3rd Northumbrian Brigade	
	D/51 " " " " 1st " "	
	D/52 " " " " 4th Durham (How^r) Brigade	
	4th Group moved back to VOLKERINCKHOVE for training	

H. T. Belcher
Lieut Col RFA.

(73989) W4141—463. 400,000. 9/14. H.&J.Ltd. Forms/C. 2118/10.

9th Divisional Artillery

53rd Bde. R. F. A.

J A N U A R Y, 1 9 1 6.

Instructions regarding War Diaries and Intelligence Summaries are contained in F. S. Regs., Part II. and the Staff Manual respectively. Title pages will be prepared in manuscript.

WAR DIARY
or
INTELLIGENCE SUMMARY.
(*Erase heading not required.*)

Army Form C. 2118.

5-3rd Brigade RFA

Hour, Date, Place	Summary of Events and Information	Remarks and references to Appendices
January 7th	4th Group moved to divisional rest area at CAESTRE.	
25th - 31st	Relieved batteries of 25th D.A in the line near LE BIZET & PLOEGSTEERT. — Batteries grouped for tactics to the other Brigades	

H. T. Belcher Lieut Col

COMMANDING 53RD BRIGADE, R.F.A.

(73989) W4141—463. 400,000. 9/14. H.&J.Ltd. Forms/C. 2118/10.

9th Divisional Artillery

53rd Bde. R. F. A.

F E B R U A R Y, 1 9 1 6.

Instructions regarding War Diaries and Intelligence Summaries are contained in F. S. Regs., Part II. and the Staff Manual respectively. Title pages will be prepared in manuscript.

WAR DIARY
or
INTELLIGENCE SUMMARY.
(*Erase heading not required.*)

Army Form C. 2118.

53rd Brigade, R.F.A.

Hour, Date, Place	Summary of Events and Information	Remarks and references to Appendices
NIEPPE February 20	The 4.5 18 pr. group was dissolved & 53rd (How.) Brigade reconstituted. The batteries remained grouped with the other Brigades for tactics.	

H. T. Belcher Lieut Col

COMMANDING 53RD BRIGADE, R.F.A.

9th Divisional Artillery

53rd Bde. R. F. A.

M A R C H, 1 9 1 6.

Vol 10

Army Form C. 2118.

IX

Instructions regarding War Diaries and Intelligence Summaries are contained in F. S. Regs., Part II. and the Staff Manual respectively. Title pages will be prepared in manuscript.

WAR DIARY
or
INTELLIGENCE SUMMARY.
(Erase heading not required.)

53rd Brigade R.F.A.

Hour, Date, Place	Summary of Events and Information	Remarks and references to Appendices
1916 March at NIEPPE.	No tactical duties - batteries remained grouped with other brigades for holding the line	

H. T. Belcher.
.... LIEUT. COLONEL, R.F.A.
COMMANDING 53rd BRIGADE, R.F.A.

9th Divisional Artillery

53rd Bde. R. F. A.

A P R I L, 1 9 1 6.

Vol 11

Army Form C. 2118.

Instructions regarding War Diaries and Intelligence Summaries are contained in F. S. Regs., Part II. and the Staff Manual respectively. Title pages will be prepared in manuscript.

WAR DIARY
or
INTELLIGENCE SUMMARY.
(Erase heading not required.)

53rd Brigade R.F.A.

Hour, Date, Place	Summary of Events and Information	Remarks and references to Appendices
1916 April at NIEPPE	No tactical duties – batteries remained grouped with other brigades for holding the line	

A. T. Butcher

LIEUT. COLONEL, R.F.A.
COMMANDING [illegible] BRIGADE

9th Divisional Artillery

53rd Bde. R. F. A.

J U N E, 1 9 1 6.

June Vol 13

Army Form C. 2118.

Instructions regarding War Diaries and Intelligence Summaries are contained in F. S. Regs., Part II. and the Staff Manual respectively. Title pages will be prepared in manuscript.

IX

WAR DIARY
or
~~INTELLIGENCE SUMMARY.~~
(*Erase heading not required.*)

53 Brigade RFA

Hour, Date, Place	Summary of Events and Information	Remarks and references to Appendices
June 1	The Brigade marched from CAESTRE to MAMETZ for training in First Army area	
13.	The Brigade entrained to AMIENS going into Billets in CORBIE.	
14.	The Brigade came under control of 30th Div & moved into that divisional area.	
	Preparation of battery positions undertaken between CARNOY & MARICOURT as Forward Batteries.	
	H. I. Belcher Lt Col RFA Commanding 53 Brigade	

(73989) W4141—463. 400,000. 9/14. H.&J.Ltd. Forms/C. 2118/10.

9th Divisional Artillery

53rd Bde. R. F. A.

M A Y, 1 9 1 6.

Vol 12

IX Army Form C. 2118.

Instructions regarding War Diaries and Intelligence Summaries are contained in F. S. Regs., Part II. and the Staff Manual respectively. Title pages will be prepared in manuscript.

WAR DIARY
or
INTELLIGENCE SUMMARY.
(*Erase heading not required.*)

53rd Brigade R.F.A.

Hour, Date, Place	Summary of Events and Information	Remarks and references to Appendices
1916 at NIEPPE May 27	Brigade moved into rest in CAESTRE area on relief by 183 Brigade R.F.A.	
	H. T. Belcher Lieut. Col. RA Commanding 53 Bde.	

(73989) W4141—463. 400,000. 9/14. H.&J.Ltd. Forms/C. 2118/10.

9th Div.
XIII.Corps.

Division transferred to IV.Corps, First Army, 25.7.16.

WAR DIARY

Headquarters,

53rd BRIGADE, R.F.A.

J U L Y

1 9 1 6

9 Sally

Army Form C. 2118.

Instructions regarding War Diaries and Intelligence Summaries are contained in F. S. Regs., Part II. and the Staff Manual respectively. Title pages will be prepared in manuscript.

WAR DIARY
or
~~INTELLIGENCE SUMMARY~~.
(*Erase heading not required.*)

53rd Brigade ~~RFA~~ Vol 14

Hour, Date, Place	Summary of Events and Information	Remarks and references to Appendices
July 1	Batteries in action near Maricourt, unbrigaded under 30th D.A. – Employed during preliminary bombardment cutting wire on support lines – afterwards bombarding Montauban in conjunction with 30th D.A & forming a barrage beyond the village while it was being consolidated. Firing was continuous for 24 hours during which time batteries had each fired about 3500 rounds.	
July 2 – 6	Batteries kept constant fire on the hostile second line in the neighbourhood of Longueval.	
July 5	The Brigade assumed tactical control of A/53. B/53. C/53. B/57 & D/52.	
July 7	[illegible], B/53, C/53 moved forward into positions S.E. of Montauban – all three batteries in line.	
July 8	B/57 & D/52 rejoined their Brigades on moving forward.	
July 9	B/53 & C/53 were unable to remain in their positions owing to shell fire – they withdrew to positions in rear of GLATZ Redoubt. A/53 prepared a new position near the redoubt.	
July 10 – 13	B/53 & C/53 cutting wire on hostile second line at S.E. corner of Longueval village. A/53 firing on hostile second line at night to keep wire open.	

(73989) W4141—463. 400,000. 9/14. H.&J.Ltd. Forms/C. 2118/10.

Instructions regarding War Diaries and Intelligence Summaries are contained in F. S. Regs., Part II. and the Staff Manual respectively. Title pages will be prepared in manuscript.

WAR DIARY
or
INTELLIGENCE SUMMARY.
(*Erase heading not required.*)

Army Form C. 2118.

58 Brigade R.F.A.

Page 2.

Hour, Date, Place	Summary of Events and Information	Remarks and references to Appendices
July 13	A/53 moved forward to position prepared near Glatz Redoubt. Brigade H.Q. moved to dugouts in same neighbourhood.	
July 14 3-20 am.	Supported attack by our Infantry on hostile second line and Longueval village by series of barrages through the village & through Delville wood. Fire continued up to 4 pm.	
	By the end of this day the Brigade had only half its guns in action owing to trouble with recoil mechanism.	
July 16	Batteries moved into positions in the open on N. slopes of the valley between Longueval & Montauban facing N.E. in the direction of Guinchy.	
	Brigade H.Q. moved to a quarry at N.W. corner of Bernafay wood	
July 16 – 26	When no operations were in progress, continual fire was kept on country E & N.E. of Delville wood by one battery at a time firing at the rate of 40 rounds per hour day & night.	
July 22 1.55 am to 3.45 am	The Brigade formed barrages in Guillemont village to support an attack by 3rd Div. on trenches S.E. of Delville Wood.	

Instructions regarding War Diaries and Intelligence Summaries are contained in F. S. Regs., Part II. and the Staff Manual respectively. Title pages will be prepared in manuscript.

WAR DIARY
or
INTELLIGENCE SUMMARY.
(Erase heading not required.)

Army Form C. 2118.

Page 3

Hour, Date, Place	Summary of Events and Information	Remarks and references to Appendices
July 23 3·40am.	3rd Div attacked Guillemont Station; ~~[illegible]~~ in support of this attack the Brigade formed barrages at W. exits of Guinchy.	
July 27 6·10am	Brigade supported attack on Longueval & Delville wood by forming barrages E of the wood. Liason formed, for this operation, with 99th I. B.	
	Firing continued until 8·0pm.	
Night of July 27/28	Brigade withdrew to wagon lines near Bray. No brigade came in to take its place.	
July 28	Brigade marched to Vaux-sur-Somme	
July 29	Brigade marched to Poulainville	
July 30	Brigade marched to Condé-Folie.	
	From July 16 until the Brigade was withdrawn, batteries & Brigade HQ. were subjected at intervals to heavy but unaimed fire by all natures of guns & Howitzers	

(73989) W4141—463. 400,000. 9/14. H.&J.Ltd. Forms/C. 2118/10.

Instructions regarding War Diaries and Intelligence Summaries are contained in F. S. Regs., Part II. and the Staff Manual respectively. Title pages will be prepared in manuscript.

WAR DIARY
or
INTELLIGENCE SUMMARY.
(Erase heading not required.)

Army Form C. 2118.

53 Brigade RFA

Hour, Date, Place	Summary of Events and Information	Remarks and references to Appendices
	Page 4	
	During the period July 1 – 28 each battery fired approximately 20,000 rounds.	
	Casualties suffered by the Brigade during the operations:—	
	Killed. Officers — 2	
	O.R. — 19	
	Wounded Officers — 7	
	O.R. — 98	
	One F.O.O. was maintained by the brigade – each battery assisting. On July 1 & July 14 there was an intermediate station under an officer to assist the F.O.O. in keeping connection with the Brigade	

H.T. Belcher.
Lt Col RFA
Commanding 53 Brigade

9th Divisional Artillery

53rd Bde. R. F. A.

A U G U S T, 1 9 1 6.

53rd Bde RFA

Army Form C. 2118.

Vol 15

Instructions regarding War Diaries and Intelligence Summaries are contained in F. S. Regs., Part II. and the Staff Manual respectively. Title pages will be prepared in manuscript.

WAR DIARY
or
INTELLIGENCE SUMMARY.

(*Erase heading not required.*)

Hour, Date, Place	Summary of Events and Information	Remarks and references to Appendices
August 1st	Brigade marched to LONGPRÉ and entrained there. Detrained at BRIAS and marched to MAREST_	
	Resting at MAREST	
August 13th	Brigade marched to GAUCHIN LEGAL via. BOURSE DEVAL, LA COMTÉ _ wagon lines at GAUCHIN LEGAL	
Night 13/14th	~~ONE~~ section of A/53 + B/53 relieve corresponding sections of 126 Brigade 37th Div._	
August 14th	Night of 14/15 remaining sections of A/53 + B/53	

Instructions regarding War Diaries and Intelligence Summaries are contained in F. S. Regs., Part II. and the Staff Manual respectively. Title pages will be prepared in manuscript.

WAR DIARY
or
~~INTELLIGENCE~~ SUMMARY.
(Erase heading not required.)

Army Form C. 2118.

Hour, Date, Place	Summary of Events and Information	Remarks and references to Appendices
August 14th	Relieve their corresponding sections of 126 Bde	
	C/53 is attached to 51st Brigade for Tasks (Right Group)	
Aug. 15th	Relief is completed. ~~the~~ 53 Brigade H.Q with their wagon lines move up to BOIS de BOUVIGNY	
	53 Brigade from reserve Brigade to the Left Group	
	B/53 in position Eastern extremity of BOIS de BOUVIGNY	
	A/53 in position N of ABLAIN St NAZAIRE	

(73989) W4141—463. 400,000. 9/14. H.&J.Ltd. Forms/C. 2118/10.

Instructions regarding War Diaries and Intelligence Summaries are contained in F. S. Regs., Part II. and the Staff Manual respectively. Title pages will be prepared in manuscript.

WAR DIARY
or
~~INTELLIGENCE~~ SUMMARY.
(Erase heading not required.)

Army Form C. 2118.

Hour, Date, Place	Summary of Events and Information	Remarks and references to Appendices
August 15th 15	Brigade in action Holding the line East of CARENCY	
August 28th		
August 29th	One section of B/53 take over from corresponding section of C/316, with their guns at a position W of BOIS de BERTHONVAL	
August 30th	Remaining Section of B/53 take over from C/316 - Relief is completed + command changes hands at 6.30 PM. B/53 becomes Technically under command of 63rd Division.	

Army Form C. 2118.

Instructions regarding War Diaries and Intelligence Summaries are contained in F. S. Regs., Part II. and the Staff Manual respectively. Title pages will be prepared in manuscript.

WAR DIARY

or

~~INTELLIGENCE SUMMARY~~.

(*Erase heading not required.*)

Hour, Date, Place	Summary of Events and Information	Remarks and references to Appendices
August 31st	At 9 AM today A/53 becomes tactically under the command of 52 Brigade.	
	H. T. Belcher Lieut Col Comdg 53rd Brigade R.F.A.	

(73989) W4141—463. 400,000. 9/14. H.&J.Ltd. Forms/C. 2118/10.

R.A.,
9th Division

No 35A AUG. 31st 1916

Herewith WAR DIARY of 53rd Brigade. R.F.A. for month of AUGUST 1916.

Please acknowledge receipt.

C H Spragge 2Lt. R.F.A.

ADJUTANT,
53RD BRIGADE, R.F.A.

9th Divisional Artillery

53rd Bde. R. F. A.

S E P T E M B E R, 1 9 1 6.

Broken up in September:
53rd Bde.H.Q. became H.Q.
52nd Bde.
Batteries absorbed by
50th & 51st Bdes.

Broken up in September.

53rd Bde RFA

Army Form C. 2118.

Vol 16

Instructions regarding War Diaries and Intelligence Summaries are contained in F. S. Regs., Part II. and the Staff Manual respectively. Title pages will be prepared in manuscript.

WAR DIARY
or
~~INTELLIGENCE~~ SUMMARY.

(*Erase heading not required.*)

Hour, Date, Place	Summary of Events and Information	Remarks and references to Appendices
August 31st	At 9 AM today A/53 becomes tactically under the command of the 52nd Brigade –	
August 31st to Sept 11th	Holding the line	
Sept 11th	53rd Brigade Staff take over and become HQ of 52 Brigade under the new reorganization – Batteries of the 53rd Brigade become absorbed in the 51st + 50th Brigades. –	

(73989) W4141—463. 400,000. 9/14. H.&J.Ltd. Forms/C. 2118/10.

Instructions regarding War Diaries and Intelligence Summaries are contained in F. S. Regs., Part II. and the Staff Manual respectively. Title pages will be prepared in manuscript.

WAR DIARY
or
INTELLIGENCE SUMMARY.
(Erase heading not required.)

Army Form C. 2118.

Hour, Date, Place	Summary of Events and Information	Remarks and references to Appendices
Sept 11th	~~The~~ A/53 becomes 51st Brigade, but for Tactical reasons remain where it is and Tactically under command of 52 Bde. One section becomes A/51 the other B/51	
	B/53 are absorbed in the 50 Brigade - a section to A/50 & a section to B/50	
	C/53 are absorbed in the 51st Brigade -	
	H.T. Belcher Lieut Col Comd'g 53 Brigade RFA	
	Closed - 11-9-16	

(73989) W4141—463. 400,000. 9/14. H.&J.Ltd. Forms/C. 2118/10.

9TH DIVISION

9TH DIVL AMMN COLUMN

MAY 1915 - ~~DEC 1918~~ 1919 SEP

9th Division

121/7598

K

9th D.A.C.

Vol I

May to Oct. 15.

HEADQUARTERS

9th DIVISIONAL Ammunition COLUMN

MAY to OCTOBER

1915

CONFIDENTIAL

WARDIARY

of

9th Divisional Ammunition Column

From 18th May 1915 To 31st October 1915

VOLUME I

Instructions regarding War Diaries and Intelligence Summaries are contained in F. S. Regs., Part II. and the Staff Manual respectively. Title pages will be prepared in manuscript.

WAR DIARY
or
INTELLIGENCE SUMMARY.
(*Erase heading not required.*)

Army Form C. 2118.

Hour, Date, Place 1915	Summary of Events and Information	Remarks and references to Appendices
11 am May 7th BORDON	Received orders to mobilise.	No Mobilization Store Table [illegible] until 6 hours after order to mobilize received.
6 pm May 11th BORDON	Column [illegible] to entrain - moved in 5 trains.	
May 12 SOUTHAMPTON	Embarked on 5 different ships, mixed up with other units	
May 13th HAVRE	Disembarked at various times & again entrained in 5 trains.	
May 14	Last train left HAVRE - 12.23	
May 15 ST OMER	Detrained at ST OMER & marched to TILQUES - 2½ miles - and billeted.	
3 pm May 15th TILQUES	Marched to STEYVER - 4½ miles - [illegible]	
May 17 STEYVER	[illegible]	
9 am May 18	Marched to METEREN - 16 miles. Heavy rain.	
May 19 METEREN	Halt. HQ in billets, remainder in bivouac.	
May 27	No 3 Section marched to STEENWERCK [illegible]	
19th - 31st May METEREN	Halt	
June 1st		
June 4	Halt.	
7 pm June 5th METEREN	Marched to HAMES-ARTOIS 18 [illegible]	
8 am June 6 HAMES-ARTOIS	No 1 & 2 Sections arrived - HQ [illegible] in billets - [illegible] in bivouac.	
June 8th	No 3 Section arrived & were billeted at FERFAY	
June 8 - 25	Halt	
June 25th BOURECQ	Marched to BOURECQ - 3 miles in very heavy rain. [illegible]	
June 25 - 28	Halt	
June 28th LE VERTANNOY	Marched to LE VERTANNOY 8 miles - all [illegible]	
June 29 ROBECQ	HQ, 2 & 3 Sections to ROBECQ [illegible] to [illegible]	

(73989) W4141—463. 400,000. 9/14. H.&J.Ltd. Forms/C. 2118/10.

Army Form C. 2118.

Instructions regarding War Diaries and Intelligence Summaries are contained in F. S. Regs., Part II. and the Staff Manual respectively. Title pages will be prepared in manuscript.

WAR DIARY
or
INTELLIGENCE SUMMARY.
(Erase heading not required.)

Hour, Date, Place 1915		Summary of Events and Information	Remarks and references to Appendices
June 29. 30	ROBECQ	Halt, men in bivouacs.	
July 1-2	"	Halt.	
July 2	RIEZ du VINAGE	Marched to RIEZ DU VINAGE 1½ miles, men in bivouacs.	
July 2-31	"	Halt. No water [illegible] which was left to issue ammunition regularly to B.A.C. distant about 6 miles.	Great shortage of drinking water
1 am July 29	RIEZ	Explosion of [illegible] in guard tent [illegible] 2 drivers [illegible] 2 being seriously injured.	
August 1-15	RIEZ du VINAGE	Halt.	
2 pm August 15	CANTRAINNE	Marched to CANTRAINNE 7 miles.	
August 15-31	"	Halt, men mostly in bivouacs.	
Sept 1. 2	"		
[illegible] Sept 2	ANNEZIN	Marched to ANNEZIN 8 miles.	
[illegible]		Halt [illegible] in bivouacs.	
Sept 6-20		Halt.	
[illegible] Sept 21		Bombardment [illegible] allowance of ammunition [illegible] 150 rounds per 18 pr gun per day [illegible] ammunition [illegible]	
		Park [illegible] was established at ANNEZIN [illegible] charge of [illegible]	
Sept 23		[illegible] the night [illegible]	
		Making changes [illegible]	

(73989) W4141—463. 400,000. 9/14. H.&J.Ltd. Forms/C. 2118/10.

Army Form C. 2118.

Instructions regarding War Diaries and Intelligence Summaries are contained in F. S. Regs., Part II. and the Staff Manual respectively. Title pages will be prepared in manuscript.

WAR DIARY
or
INTELLIGENCE SUMMARY.
(*Erase heading not required.*)

Hour, Date, Place	Summary of Events and Information	Remarks and references to Appendices
1915		
6.30 am Sept 25. ANNEZIN	Attack on enemy's lines — the rain having softened the roads [illegible] [illegible] [illegible] [illegible] [illegible]. In spite of many [illegible] [illegible] [illegible] having been dumped the ground in the camp was a foot deep in mud.	
Sept 26–29 ANNEZIN	Carrying of ammunition & hand grenades constantly [illegible] [illegible] [illegible] [illegible]	
October 1st STEENWERCK	Marched to STEENWERCK [illegible] [illegible] [illegible]	
Oct 2nd POPERINGHE	Marched to POPERINGHE 10½ miles	
Oct 3–31	Halt [illegible] [illegible] [illegible] [illegible]	[illegible signature]

(73989) W4141—463. 400,000. 9/14. H.&J.Ltd. Forms/C. 2118/10.

9th Division

9th D.A.C.
Vol. 2

Nov.
Dec. } 1915.

/21
7910

12

HEADQUARTERS

9TH DIVISIONAL AMMUNITION COLUMN

NOVEMBER ... DECEMBER

1915

Army Form C. 2118.

Instructions regarding War Diaries and Intelligence Summaries are contained in F. S. Regs., Part II. and the Staff Manual respectively. Title pages will be prepared in manuscript.

WAR DIARY
or
INTELLIGENCE SUMMARY.
(Erase heading not required.)

Hour, Date, Place	Summary of Events and Information	Remarks and references to Appendices
1-21 December 1915 near POPERINGHE	Halt - men in billets & huts. Weather very bad - incessant rain.	
21st December	No 2 section marched to BORRE - relieving section of 50 DAC.	
22nd December	Remainder of Column marched to BORRE into rest billets. March 14 miles in bad weather - Column accommodated in billets except of one section in bivouacs	
26 December	Billets of section in bivouac having been disinfected, all column in billets	
23-31.	Halt BORRE.	

[illegible signature]
Lt Col
Comdt 9 DAC

15

9 D.A.C.

Instructions regarding War Diaries and Intelligence Summaries are contained in F. S. Regs., Part II. and the Staff Manual respectively. Title pages will be prepared in manuscript.

WAR DIARY
or
~~INTELLIGENCE~~ SUMMARY.
(Erase heading not required.)

Army Form C. 2118.

Hour, Date, Place	Summary of Events and Information	Remarks and references to Appendices
1st to 30th November near POPERINGHE	Halt. men in billets, bivouacs + tents	

[illegible]
[illegible]
Cmdt 9 D.A.C.

9th Divisional Artillery

9th DIVISIONAL AMMUNITION COLUMN,

J A N U A R Y, 1 9 1 6.

Confidential.

War Diary

of

9th Divisional Ammunition Column.

From January 1st 1916 January 31st 1916.

Volume III.

19

Instructions regarding War Diaries and Intelligence Summaries are contained in F. S. Regs., Part II. and the Staff Manual respectively. Title pages will be prepared in manuscript.

WAR DIARY
or
INTELLIGENCE SUMMARY.
(*Erase heading not required.*)

Army Form C. 2118.

Hour, Date, Place	Summary of Events and Information	Remarks and references to Appendices
January 1-31- 1916 BORRE	Halt - men in billets.	
	4/2/16 [illegible] [illegible] [illegible]	

(73989) W4141—463. 400,000. 9/14. H.&J.Ltd. Forms/C. 2118/10.

22

9th Divisional Artillery

9th DIVISIONAL AMMUNITION COLUMN,

F E B R U A R Y, 1 9 1 6.

Confidential.

War Diary

of

The 9th Divisional Ammunition Column R.F.A.

From Feb 1st 1916. To Feb 29th 1916

Volume.

Instructions regarding War Diaries and Intelligence Summaries are contained in F. S. Regs., Part II. and the Staff Manual respectively. Title pages will be prepared in manuscript.

WAR DIARY
or
INTELLIGENCE SUMMARY.
(*Erase heading not required.*)

Army Form C. 2118.

Hour, Date, Place	Summary of Events and Information	Remarks and references to Appendices
1916 1-29 February BORRE	Halt. ½ section at advanced dump near NIEPPE. rem in billets.	
	Holwallin Lieut Col RFA Cmd 9 DAC	

W4141—463. 400,000. 9/14. H.&J.Ltd. Forms/C. 2118/10.

9th Divisional Artillery

9th DIVISIONAL AMMUNITION COLUMN,

A P R I L, 1 9 1 6.

9 Div
A Col
Vol 6

Confidential

War Diary of the

9th Divisional Ammunition Column R.F.A.

from April 1st 1916 to April 30th 1916.

(Volume 6)

31

Instructions regarding War Diaries and Intelligence Summaries are contained in F. S. Regs., Part II. and the Staff Manual respectively. Title pages will be prepared in manuscript.

WAR DIARY
or
INTELLIGENCE SUMMARY.
(Erase heading not required.)

Army Form C. 2118.

HEADQUARTERS No. ...... Date 30/4/16 5th DIVISIONAL AMMN. COLUMN

Hour, Date, Place	Summary of Events and Information	Remarks and references to Appendices
SCHAEXKEN 1916 April 1–30	Halt. 1½ sections at SCHAEXKEN with HQ. 1 section at LA CRECHE, ½ section MEPPE	
April 13th	No 2 section returned to SCHAEXKEN, No 1 section relieving No 2 at LA CRECHE	

[illegible]
Lieut Col RA

32

(73989) W4141—463. 400,000. 9/14. H.&J.Ltd. Forms/C. 2118/10.

9th Divisional Artillery

9th DIVISIONAL AMMUNITION COLUMN,

M A Y, 1 9 1 6.

9 DAC
Vol. 7

Confidential

War Diary

of

The Ninth Divisional Column

from May 1st 1916 to May 31st 1916.

Volume 1.

35

Instructions regarding War Diaries and Intelligence Summaries are contained in F. S. Regs., Part II. and the Staff Manual respectively. Title pages will be prepared in manuscript.

WAR DIARY
or
~~INTELLIGENCE SUMMARY.~~
(Erase heading not required.)

HEADQUARTERS * 9th DIVISIONAL COLUMN * No. Date 31/5/16

Army Form C. 2118.

Hour, Date, Place	Summary of Events and Information	Remarks and references to Appendices
May 1st – 14th	HALT – Headquarters + 2 sections at SCHAEXKEN – 3rd section at LA CRECHE	
14–15	Column re-organised into 4 sections.	
15 – 27	HQ + part of No 4 section at LA CRECHE – 1, 2, 3 sections near METEREN – remainder at SCHAEXKEN	
27	March to BORRE & surrounding villages	
28 – 31st	Halt at BORRE	

[illegible]
Lt Col RA
Comd 9 DAC

3/6/16

(73989) W4141—463. 400,000. 9/14. H.&J.Ltd. Forms/C. 2118/10.

9th Divisional Artillery

9th DIVISIONAL AMMUNITION COLUMN,

JUNE, 1916.

June 1916

Instructions regarding War Diaries and Intelligence Summaries are contained in F. S. Regs., Part II. and the Staff Manual respectively. Title pages will be prepared in manuscript.

WAR DIARY
or
~~INTELLIGENCE SUMMARY.~~
(Erase heading not required.)

HEADQUARTERS 9th DIVL. AMMN COLUMN No. 1/7/16

Army Form C. 2118.

June 9th D.A. amm col Vol 8

Hour, Date, Place	Summary of Events and Information	Remarks and references to Appendices
BORRE. 1st June 1916	Column marched to ROQUETTIRE. 17 miles. men in bivouacs.	
ROQUETTIRE. 1 – 14 June	HALT – divisional training.	
15 June	Marched to entrain. HQ & 4 sections to BERGUETTE – 1 & 2 sections to LILLERS	
16 June	Detrained at LONGEAU marched into camp at BOIS DES TAILLES near BRAY. No 4 section encamped at SAILLY LAURETTE	
17 – 27	Encamped in BOIS DES TAILLES.	
18	3 drivers of No 1 section wounded. 5 horses killed by shell fire	
21	2 gunners killed & wounded by shell fire.	
28	Marched to SAILLY LE SEC, No 4 section moving to VAUX SUR SOMME	Very heavy rain
28 – 30	HALT – SAILLY LE SEC.	

[signature]

COL. 9th DIVL. AMMN COLM.

(73989) W4141—463. 400,000. 9/14. H.&J.Ltd. Forms/C. 2118/10.

9th Divisional Artillery

9th DIVISIONAL AMMUNITION COLUMN,

MARCH, 1916.

9 Div AC
Vol 5

Confidential

War Diary of

9th Divisional Ammunition Column R F A

from March 1st 1916 to March 31st 1916

Volume 5

27

Instructions regarding War Diaries and Intelligence Summaries are contained in F. S. Regs., Part II. and the Staff Manual respectively. Title pages will be prepared in manuscript.

WAR DIARY
or
INTELLIGENCE SUMMARY.
(Erase heading not required.)

Army Form C. 2118.

Hour, Date, Place	Summary of Events and Information	Remarks and references to Appendices
1st to 7th March 1916 BORRE	Halt	
7th March	No 3 Section marched to LA CRECHE for Corps fatigues & encamped there - officers & men in huts.	
10th March	H.Q. 1 & 2 sections marched to SCHAEXKEN - about 9 miles. officers in billets. men in barns.	
11-31 March SCHAEXKEN	Halt. HQ & No 1 section at SCHAEXKEN - ½ No 2 section SCHAEXKEN remainder in camp near NIEPPE. No 3 section at LA CRECHE.	

[signature]
Lieut Col RAMC
Comdg 9 Div?

28

41

9th Div.
XIII.Corps.

Division transferred
to IV.Corps, First
Army, 25.7.16.

WAR
DIARY

9th DIVISION AMMUNITION COLUMN.

J U L Y

1 9 1 6

Instructions regarding War Diaries and Intelligence Summaries are contained in F. S. Regs., Part II. and the Staff Manual respectively. Title pages will be prepared in manuscript.

or

INTELLIGENCE SUMMARY.

(*Erase heading not required.*)

9 Div A Col

Vol 9

Place	Date	Hour	Summary of Events and Information	Remarks and references to Appendices
1916				
SAILLY-LE-SEC	1st July		HALT - A Echelon at SAILLY-LE-SEC - B Echelon at VAUX-SUR-SOMME - all in bivouacs - commenced sending ammunition up to battery positions daily from A echelon + 20 wagons daily from B echelon for stone fatigues under C.R.E.	
	7/July		1 driver killed by shell fire -	
BOIS DES TAILLES	9/July		Marched to BOIS DES TAILLES with A echelon - B echelon moving into SAILLY-LE-SEC	
	11/July		1 driver wounded by shell fire	
	12/July		2 drivers " "	
	13/July		1 driver " "	
	16/July		1 driver killed, 7 wounded by shell fire	
	17/July		1 officer gassed (Lieut GUY)	
GROVETOWN	18/July		A+B echelons marched to GROVETOWN.	
	20/July		8 drivers wounded by shell fire.	
VAUX-SUR-SOMME	28/July		A+B echelons marched to VAUX-SUR-SOMME.	
ALLONVILLE	29/July		Column marched to ALLONVILLE	
BOUCHON	30/July		Column marched to L'ETOILE + BOUCHON. No 1 Section to CONDE FOLIE, No 3 Section to LONG	

H. L. Walker
Lieut Col RA
Comm 9 D.A.C.

42

T2134. Wt. W708-776. 500000. 4/15. Sir J. C. & S.

44

9th Divisional Artillery

9th DIVISIONAL AMMUNITION COLUMN,

A U G U S T, 1 9 1 6.

Instructions regarding War Diaries and Intelligence Summaries are contained in F. S. Regs., Part II. and the Staff Manual respectively. Title pages will be prepared in manuscript.

WAR DIARY
or
INTELLIGENCE SUMMARY.
(Erase heading not required.)

~~9~~ Army Form C. 2118.

VOL 10

Place	Date	Hour	Summary of Events and Information	Remarks and references to Appendices
LONGRRE / PONT REMY	1 Aug	6 a.m. to 2 o p.m.	Column entrained for BRYAS and DIEVAL – marched from thence to MAGNICOURT-EN-COMTE	
MAGNICOURT	1 Aug to 9 Aug		Halt at MAGNICOURT – all ranks in tents or bivouacs.	
HOUVELIN	10 Aug		Marched to HOUVELIN – No 2 Section to DIVION	
HOUVELIN and DIVION	10 Aug to 12 Aug		Halt at HOUVELIN and DIVION	
CAUCOURT and HERIPRE	13 Aug		Marched to CAUCOURT and HERIPRE – No 4 Section at HERIPRE – No 2 Section HERMIN. Rest being in tents at CAUCOURT until departure of 37 D.C. – ARP formed, under Lieut SKELTON near GRAND SERVINS.	
do	17 Aug		No 2 Section marched in from HERMIN	
ditto	17–31 Aug		Halt at CAUCOURT & HERMIN	

[signature] LIEUT. COL. R.F.A.
O.C. 9th DIVL. COLN.

T2134. Wt. W708-776. 500000. 4/15. Sir J. C. & S.

45

9th Divisional Artillery

9th DIVISIONAL AMMUNITION COLUMN,

S E P T E M B E R, 1 9 1 6.

Instructions regarding War Diaries and Intelligence Summaries are contained in F. S. Regs., Part II. and the Staff Manual respectively. Title pages will be prepared in manuscript.

WAR DIARY
or
INTELLIGENCE SUMMARY.
(Erase heading not required.)

HEADQUARTERS No. .... Date 1.10.16. 9th DIVISIONAL COLUMN

Army Form C. 2118.

9th D A C

Vol 11

Place	Date	Hour	Summary of Events and Information	Remarks and references to Appendices
[illegible]	September 1st – 30th		Headquarters & No 1, 2 & 3 Sections } Hall. M/sm in billets & bivouacs	
			1 officer & 20 men at GRAND SERVINS A.R.P.	
HERIPRÉ	"		No 4 Section	
			2 officers 150 men Trench tramway work at Mt St ELOI	

Jue Hall LIEUT.-COL., R.F.A.
O.C. 9th DIVISIONAL COLUMN.

T2134. Wt. W708–776. 500000. 4/15. Sir J. C. & S.

48

50

9th Divisional Artillery

9th DIVISIONAL AMMUNITION COLUMN,

O C T O B E R, 1 9 1 6.

9th D.A.C

Instructions regarding War Diaries and Intelligence Summaries are contained in F. S. Regs., Part II, and the Staff Manual respectively. Title pages will be prepared in manuscript.

WAR DIARY
or
INTELLIGENCE SUMMARY.
(Erase heading not required.)

HEADQUARTERS No. Dated 5/10/16 9th DIVISIONAL COLUMN

Army Form C. 2118.

Vol 12

Place	Date	Hour	Summary of Events and Information	Remarks and references to Appendices
	Oct 1916			
CAUCOURT	1-4		Halt. Men in billets.	
" "	5		Column marched to MAGNICOURT. Men in billets	
MAGNICOURT	5-8		Halt. Column marched to REBREUVIETTE on morning of the 8th.	
REBREUVIETTE	9		Column continued it's march to GROUCHES.	
GROUCHES	10		Halted for night 9/10 October and marched to VILLERS BOCAGE on morning of 10th.	
VILLERS BOCAGE	11		Halted for night of 10/11 Oct and marched to BEHENCOURT morning of 11th.	
BEHENCOURT	11-13		Halt. Men in billets. Advance party went on to take over Camps. &c. &c. Column marched on 13th.	
BECOURT	13		Arrived at BECOURT. Sections halting and encamping near BECOURT HILL. Headqrs proceeded to valley just S. of MAMETZ WOOD (close to A.R.P. Headqrs stayed here until morning of 15th when it marched back to BECOURT and encamped just S of BECOURT WOOD.	
	15-31		HQ remained encamped S of BECOURT WOOD. Sections on BECOURT HILL. Men in bivouacs.	

Fred Hall LIEUT.-COL. R.F.A.
O.C. 9th DIVISIONAL COLUMN.

T2134. Wt. W708-776. 500000. 4/15. Sir J. C. & S.

5

9th Divisional Artillery

9th DIVISIONAL AMMUNITION COLUMN,

N O V E M B E R, 1 9 1 6.

9th DAC

Instructions regarding War Diaries and Intelligence Summaries are contained in F. S. Regs., Part II. and the Staff Manual respectively. Title pages will be prepared in manuscript.

WAR DIARY
or
~~INTELLIGENCE SUMMARY.~~
(Erase heading not required.)

HEADQUARTERS Date 1/12/16 9th DIVISIONAL COL.

Army Form C. 2118.

Vol 13

Place	Date	Hour	Summary of Events and Information	Remarks and references to Appendices
BECOURT.	1-11-16 to 24-11-16		Headqrs, No1, 2, 3 & 4 Sections Halt at BECOURT HILL (South) Detachment of 30 men at. A.R.P. at BOTTOM WOOD DUMP.	
	10/11/16		2 men attached to D/51 Bde killed by Shell fire.	
	13/11/16		Shells dropped into camp of No 2 Section. 2 men wounded	
	17-11-16		Headqrs moved to new position on main road close to ALBERT.	
			Sections moved to new position on 17-11-16 and 18-11-16. New position adjoined Headqrs.	
BEHENCOURT	24-11-16		Column Marched to BEHENCOURT and halted. Men in billets.	
TALMAS.	27-11-16		March continued to TALMAS. Halt for the night	
BARLY.	28-11-16		Marched to BARLY. and halted for the night	
REBREUVIETTE	29-11-16 to 30-11-16		Marched to REBREUVIETTE and halted. Men in billets	

Fred Hall LIEUT.-COL., R.F.A.
C.C. 9th DIVISIONAL COLUMN.

56

9th Divisional Artillery

9th DIVISIONAL AMMUNITION COLUMN,

D E C E M B E R, 1 9 1 6.

9th D A C

Instructions regarding War Diaries and Intelligence Summaries are contained in F. S. Regs., Part II. and the Staff Manual respectively. Title pages will be prepared in manuscript.

WAR DIARY
or
~~INTELLIGENCE SUMMARY.~~
(Erase heading not required.)

HEADQUARTERS No. .... Date 1-1-17 9th DIVISIONAL COLUMN

Army Form C. 2118.

Vol 14

Place	Date	Hour	Summary of Events and Information	Remarks and references to Appendices
	1916			
REBREUVIETTE	Dec 1 to Dec 27.		Halted at REBREUVIETTE. Men billeted in barns &c.	
WANQUETIN	Dec 27 to Dec 31.		Marched to WANQUETIN. Men ~~in~~ billeted in huts and barns. Horses on prepared Standings. A detachment of One Officer + 40 men at Divisional Bomb Store, DUISANS.	

Fred Hall LIEUT.-COL., R.F.A.
O.C. 9th DIVISIONAL COLUMN.

T2134. Wt. W708-776. 500000. 4/15. Sir J. C. & S.

DAC

Instructions regarding War Diaries and Intelligence Summaries are contained in F. S. Regs., Part II. and the Staff Manual respectively. Title pages will be prepared in manuscript.

WAR DIARY
or
INTELLIGENCE SUMMARY.
(*Erase heading not required.*)

HEADQUARTERS No. 31 Date 1/1/17 9th DIVISIONAL COLUMN

Army Form C. 2118.

Vol 15

59

Hour, Date, Place	Summary of Events and Information	Remarks and references to Appendices
January 1.1.17 to 22.1.17	REST AT WANQUETIN Men in huts and billets Horses & mules under cover	
15.1.17	Reorganization of D.A.C. 52nd A. Field Artillery Brigade Amm Column formed from their No 2 Section 9th D.A.C. D.A.C. now consisting of "A" Echelon, composed of HQ No 1 & No 2 Sections and "B" Echelon	
22.1.17	"A" Echelon moved to FREVIN CAPELLE "B" " BRAY.	
22.1.17 – 31.1.17	Men of "A" Echelon in Huts and billets "B" Echelon in Barns. Horses & mules under cover in "A" Echelon In "B" Echelon majority of Animals under cover	

Fred Hall
Lieut. Col., R.F.A.
O.C. 9th Div. Amm. Column.

(73989) W4141—463. 400,000. 9/14. H.&J.Ltd. Forms/C. 2118/10.

9th D.A.C.

Instructions regarding War Diaries and Intelligence Summaries are contained in F. S. Regs., Part II. and the Staff Manual respectively. Title pages will be prepared in manuscript.

WAR DIARY
or
INTELLIGENCE SUMMARY.
(Erase heading not required.)

Army Form C. 2118.

Vol 16

Hour, Date, Place	Summary of Events and Information	Remarks and references to Appendices
February 1.2.17 to 10.2.17	Men of A echelon at FREVIN-CAPELLE in huts and billets. Men of B echelon at BRAY in barns remaining there the whole of the month.	
11.2.17	A echelon moved from FREVIN-CAPELLE as follows: Headquarters at LARISSET. Men in huts, animals under cover. Nos 1 + 2 Sections moved to OURTON near BRUAY. Men in barns &c	
19.2.17	Nos 1 + 2 Sections moved to MONCHEY-BRETON with orders to march to LARISSET on 21/2/17.	
20.2.17	Nos 1 + 2 Sections move to LARISSET cancelled and they ~~moved back~~ marched to PERNES remaining there the remainder of the month.	
27.2.17	One man working at Div. Bomb Stores wounded by Shell fire.	

Fred Hall
LIEUT.-COL., R.F.A.
O.C. 9th DIVISIONAL COLUMN.

(73989) W4141—463. 400,000. 9/14. H.&J.Ltd. Forms/C. 2118/10.

8

9th DAC

Instructions regarding War Diaries and Intelligence Summaries are contained in F. S. Regs., Part II. and the Staff Manual respectively. Title pages will be prepared in manuscript.

WAR DIARY
or
INTELLIGENCE SUMMARY.
(*Erase heading not required.*)

HEADQUARTERS 9th DIVISIONAL COLUMN No. ... Date 31-3-17

Army Form C. 2118.

Vol 17

Hour, Date, Place	Summary of Events and Information	Remarks and references to Appendices
March 1917. 1.3.17 to 14.3.17	B Echelon moved from BRAY to MAROEUIL on 1-3-17. and horses under cover.	Men in huts
	Headqrs at LARISSET Nos 1+2 Sections at PERNES	
14.3.17	Nos 1+2 Sections marched from PERNES to LARESSET. ~~and~~ Officers and men accommodated in large Marquees and tents (C.S.L)	
21.3.17	B Echelon marched from MAROEUIL to LARESSET.	
22-3-17 to 31-3-17	Headqrs and "A" + "B" Echelon remained at LARESSET.	
	All available horses + wagons engaged in carrying to Battery positions.	Ammunition up
28.3.17	One man attached 64th Coy R.E. killed by shell fire.	

[signature] LIEUT.-COL. R.F.A. C.O. 9th DIVISIONAL COLUMN.

(73989) W4141—463. 400,000. 9/14. H.&J.Ltd. Forms/C. 2118/10.

9th D A C

Army Form C. 2118.

Instructions regarding War Diaries and Intelligence Summaries are contained in F. S. Regs., Part II. and the Staff Manual respectively. Title pages will be prepared in manuscript.

WAR DIARY
or
INTELLIGENCE SUMMARY.
(Erase heading not required.)

Vol 18

62

Place	Date	Hour	Summary of Events and Information	Remarks and references to Appendices
LARISSET	1st/17 to 7th/17		Column at LARISSET. Engaged in carrying Ammunition from two 17th Corps Dumps to gun positions	
	8-4-17.		Column moved to MAROIEUL and bivouacked close to Railway.	
MAROEUIL	9-4-17		Remained at MAROIEUL until 5 pm. when the whole of the Column moved to ANZIN. Move was carried out in a heavy snow storm.	
ANZIN	10-4-17 to 30-4-17		Column remained at ANZIN and was engaged in carrying Ammunition to gun positions. On various dates German Guns that had been captured were brought from their positions into Camp. Quantities of ammunition were also collected.	
			Captured guns included:- 7. 7.7cm guns; 1. 9cm. gun; 5 5.9" Hows; 1 10.5cm How.	
	19-4-17		2/Lieut. A DELVES was wounded whilst collecting these guns.	
	23-4-17		Two drivers wounded whilst taking ammunition to Battery positions.	

T. M. Hall
LIEUT.-COL., R.F.A.
O.C. 9th DIVISIONAL COLUMN.

9th DAC

Instructions regarding War Diaries and Intelligence Summaries are contained in F. S. Regs., Part II. and the Staff Manual respectively. Title pages will be prepared in manuscript.

WAR DIARY
or
INTELLIGENCE SUMMARY.
(Erase heading not required.)

9th Div Am Col

Vol 19

Army Form C. 2118.

HEADQUARTERS 9th DIVISIONAL COLUMN 31/5/17

Place	Date	Hour	Summary of Events and Information	Remarks and references to Appendices
ANZIN	1.5.17 to 31/5/17		Column encamped at ANZIN. Artillery in action the whole of the month and the normal supply of Ammunition taken up to guns.	
	18/5/17		Two drivers killed and one wounded transporting ammunition to Battery position	
	3/5/17		One driver killed and Two wounded (one has since died) transporting Ammunition	

H.J. Ozanne Lieut
for LIEUT-COL, R.F.A.
O.C. 9th DIVISIONAL COLUMN.

63

T2134. Wt. W708-776. 500000. 4/15. Sir J. C. & S.

9th DAC

...s regarding War Diaries and Intelligence ...mmaries are contained in F. S. Regs., Part II. and the Staff Manual respectively. Title pages will be prepared in manuscript.

WAR DIARY
or
~~INTELLIGENCE SUMMARY~~.
(Erase heading not required.)

Army Form C. 2118.

9 D Am Col

9th DIVISIONAL COLUMN 30/6/17

Vol 20

Place	Date	Hour	Summary of Events and Information	Remarks and references to Appendices
ANZIN	1.6.17 to 27.6.17		Column remained encamped at ANZIN. Artillery in action. Normal supply of Ammunition taken up to Batteries. Column G.S. wagons engaged in Clearing old Battery positions of Ammunition and Empty Cartridge cases.	
	27.6.17		Column moved to new area. Headquarters established at AGNY and Sections between ACHICOURT and BEAVRAINS. at M.4 a (Sheet 51 B.) Large Ammunition Dump at X roads at M.4 c.1.9.	

Fred Hall Lieut. Col., R.F.A.
O.C. 9th Divisional Column.

T2134. Wt. W708–776. 500000. 4/15. Sir J. C. & S.

64

9th DAC

Instructions regarding War Diaries and Intelligence Summaries are contained in F. S. Regs., Part II. and the Staff Manual respectively. Title pages will be prepared in manuscript.

WAR DIARY
or
~~INTELLIGENCE SUMMARY~~.
(Erase heading not required.)

Army Form C. 2118.

HEADQUARTERS 1-8-17 9th DIVISIONAL COLUMN

9 D Am Col Vol 21

Place	Date	Hour	Summary of Events and Information	Remarks and references to Appendices
AGNY	1.7.17		Headquarters of Column remained at AGNY for the whole of the month of July.	
ACHICOURT	to		No1 Section and "B" Echelon remained encamped between ACHICOURT and BEAURAINS	
BEAURAINS	31.7.17		at R.34.c. and M.4.a. reference Sheet 51B	
			No2 Section who were encamped at about M.4.a. reference Sheet 51B. moved to	
			S.15.a. Sheet 51B near BOIRY-ST. MARTIN on 10/7/17 being attached for tactical	
			purposes to 21st D.A. for ammunition supply of 57th Bde R.F.A.	
			Column Wagons were engaged during the month in clearing old Battery positions	
			of Ammunition and empty cartridge cases &c	

Fred Hall LIEUT.-COL, R.F.A.
C.C. 9th DIVISIONAL COLUMN

T2134. Wt. W708-776. 500000. 4/15. Sir J. C. & S.

65

Instructions regarding War Diaries and Intelligence Summaries are contained in F. S. Regs., Part II. and the Staff Manual respectively. Title pages will be prepared in manuscript.

9 DAC

WAR DIARY
or
INTELLIGENCE SUMMARY.
(Erase heading not required.)

HEADQUARTERS 9th DIVISIONAL COLUMN No. ... Dated 1-9-17.

Army Form C. 2118.

Vol 22

Place	Date	Hour	Summary of Events and Information	Remarks and references to Appendices
AGNY.	1-8-17 to 3-8-17		Headquarters remained at AGNY. No 1. Section and 'B' Echelon at ACHICOURT and No 2 Section at BOIRY. ST. MARTIN.	
LECHELLE.	3-8-17		Column moved by March Route to LECHELLE. Headquarters encamped at FOUR WINDS FARM Sections at P.25.d (57c) and V.3.c.6.4.	
EQUANCOURT	8.8.17		No 2 Section and 'B' Echelon moved to EQUANCOURT and encamped.	
	9.8.17		No 1 Section moved to EQUANCOURT.	
	10.8.17		Headquarters moved to EQUANCOURT and encamped at the S. end of the village.	
	31.8.17		Column remained at EQUANCOURT for the whole of the month. Horse standings were built and water supply laid on to supply troughs erected in camp. Column engaged on fatigues during the month.	
	27.8.17		One man wounded by shell fire whilst on fatigues at METZ.	

Fred Hall
LIEUT.-COL., R.F.A.
O.C. 9th DIVISIONAL COLUMN

66

9th DAC

11

Army Form C. 2118.

9 D Am Col

Vol 23

Instructions regarding War Diaries and Intelligence Summaries are contained in F. S. Regs., Part II. and the Staff Manual respectively. Title pages will be prepared in manuscript.

WAR DIARY
or
~~INTELLIGENCE SUMMARY.~~
(Erase heading not required.)

HEADQUARTERS 9th DIVISIONAL COLUMN 30/9/17

Place	Date	Hour	Summary of Events and Information	Remarks and references to Appendices
EQUANCOURT	1.9.17 to 2.9.17		Column at EQUANCOURT	
BEHAGNIES	3.9.17		Marched to BEHAGNIES (near ACHIET-LE-GRAND) and encamped	
WATOU	7.9.17		Column entrained for the WATOU AREA (YPRES front). Headqrs and the S.A. Section entrained at BAPAUME Station, No 2 Section at BAPAUME (WEST) and No 1 Section at MIRAUMONT.	
			After detraining, Headqrs and sections marched independently to camp near WATOU.	
VLAMERTINGHE	10.9.17		Headqrs and advance parties from Sections marched to VLAMERTINGHE and encamped just S. of the village.	
	11.9.17		Remainder of Sections marched up from WATOU and joined advance parties.	
	12.9.17		At 1.45 pm 5 Large Bombs were dropped in No 2 Sec. lines by E.A. Four men were killed and ten wounded. Thirty six animals killed and about thirty wounded many having to be evacuated.	
POPERINGHE	15.9.17		Column moved back to camp close to POPERINGHE (G.10.d. Sheet 28)	
	18.9.17		Three men wounded whilst carrying ammunition up to Batteries. Four horses killed.	
	24.9.17 to 26.9.17		One man missing believed killed and three wounded whilst taking up ammunition.	
	29.9.17		No 89866 Sgt Allen S awarded the MILITARY MEDAL for gallantry under heavy shell fire.	
	30.9.17		From the date of arrival in this area Column engaged daily in carrying ammunition up to Battery positions.	

R Perry Capt.
for ~~Lt. Col. R.F.A.~~ Cmdg. 9th DIVISIONAL COLUMN.

Instructions regarding War Diaries and Intelligence Summaries are contained in F. S. Regs., Part II. and the Staff Manual respectively. Title pages will be prepared in manuscript.

9th D.A.C.

WAR DIARY
or
~~INTELLIGENCE SUMMARY.~~
(*Erase heading not required.*)

Army Form C. 2118.

Vol 24

Place	Date	Hour	Summary of Events and Information	Remarks and references to Appendices
POPERINGHE	1-10-17 to 5-10-17		Unit encamped at G.10.d. (Sheet 28)	
HAMHOEK	6-10-17		Column moved to billets at HAMHOEK F.24 (Sheet 27)	
VLAMERTINGHE	9-10-17		Column moved to H.4.a (Sheet 28) and encamped	
	11-10-17		One Mule killed by shellfire.	
	12-10-17		One Driver wounded and three mules killed by shell fire.	
	13-10-17		One Driver and one mule killed by shell fire.	
	15-10-17		Three Drivers wounded and two mules killed by shell fire.	
	16-10-17		One Driver and one Mule killed by shell fire.	
	17-10-17		One Sergt and one Driver wounded by shell fire.	
	19 & 20-10-17		2/Lieut Watson & 2/Lieut C Fahy wounded in action on the 19th & 20th respectively whilst attached to 51st Bde RFA.	
POPERINGHE	20-10-17		Column marched to the staging area E. of POPERINGHE and occupied billets.	
WORMHOUDT	21-10-17		Column marched to the WORMHOUDT area.	
GHYVELDE	23-10-17		Column marched to the GHYVELDE area and occupied billets.	
COXYDE	29-10-17		Column marched to COXYDE area and occupied billets. Headqrs at X.7.d.28. Good stabling and accommodation for the men.	

[signature] for LIEUT. COL., R.F.A.
O.C. 9th DIVISIONAL COLUMN

Instructions regarding War Diaries and Intelligence Summaries are contained in F. S. Regs., Part II. and the Staff Manual respectively. Title pages will be prepared in manuscript.

WAR DIARY
or
~~INTELLIGENCE~~ SUMMARY.
(Erase heading not required.)

Army Form C. 2118.

9 D Am Col
30/11/17.
Vol 25

Place	Date	Hour	Summary of Events and Information	Remarks and references to Appendices
COXYDE	1-11-17 to 20-11-17		Unit remained in COXYDE area, and was engaged in clearing the area of ammunition and empty shell cases.	
GHYVELDE	21-11-17		Column marched to GHYVELDE area.	
WORMHOUDT	22 11 17		Column continued its march to WORMHOUDT area	
ZERMEZEELE	23 11 17		Column continued its march to WORMHOUDT "B" area	
BANDRINGHEM	24 11 17		Column continued its march to WARDRECQUES area	
MERCK ST. LIEVIN	25 11 17		Column continued its march to AVROULT area	
LESPINOY	26-11-17		Column marched to FRUGES area and occupied billets stabling etc in the villages of LESPINOY-SUR-CANCHE, BEAURAINVILLE and MARENLA.	
LESPINOY	30-11-17		Column remained at LESPINOY.	

A. V. Darby 2nd Lieut
for Capt. R.F.A.
O.C. 9th Divisional Column

T2134. Wt. W708-776. 500000. 4/15. Sir J. C. & S.

69

9 D.A.C.

Instructions regarding War Diaries and Intelligence Summaries are contained in F. S. Regs., Part II. and the Staff Manual respectively. Title pages will be prepared in manuscript.

WAR DIARY
or
~~INTELLIGENCE SUMMARY.~~
(*Erase heading not required.*)

31.12.17.

Army Form C. 2118.

Vol 26

Place	Date	Hour	Summary of Events and Information	Remarks and references to Appendices
LESPINOY	1.12.17		Column in the FRUGES area. Headqrs and No 2 Section at LESPINOY No 1 Section at MARENLA and SAA Section at BEAURAINVILLE.	
			Column entrained at WAVRANS and HESDIN.	
DOINGT	2.12.17		Column arrived at PERONNE detrained and marched to DOINGT.	
MARQUAIX	3.12.17		Column marched to MARQUAIX and encamped under canvas	
BUSSU	9.12.17		Column marched to BUSSU and encamped.	
	12.12.17		No 1 Section marched to METZ en COUTURE to assist 50th Bde on salvage work.	
	14.12.17		No 1 Sec less 12 teams and drivers returned to BUSSU.	
	19.12.17		SAA Sec marched to NURLU and occupied billets. Engaged on fatigues	
NURLU	31.12.17		Headqrs Nos 1 + 2 Sections marched to NURLU.	

[illegible]
Lieut-Col. R.F.A.
9th Div. Ammunition Column

T2134. Wt. W708–776. 500000. 4/15. Sir J. C. & S.

70

9th D A C

Instructions regarding War Diaries and Intelligence Summaries are contained in F. S. Regs., Part II. and the Staff Manual respectively. Title pages will be prepared in manuscript.

WAR DIARY
or
~~INTELLIGENCE~~ SUMMARY.

(Erase heading not required.)

Army Form C. 2118.

9 D Am Col

Vol 27

Place	Date	Hour	Summary of Events and Information	Remarks and references to Appendices
NURLU.	1-1-18. to 31-1-18.		Column at NURLU. SAA section in huts and horses in covered standings. Standings and Nissen huts erected for Headqrs. No's 1 and 2 sections engaged during the month in building Huts and standings. Three Lewis Guns loaned to Unit for defence against Enemy Aircraft.	

[signature] Capt
for Lieut.-Col., R.F.A.
O.C. 9th Divisional Column

T2134. Wt. W708–776. 500000. 4/15. Sir J. C. & S.

Instructions regarding War Diaries and Intelligence Summaries are contained in F. S. Regs., Part II. and the Staff Manual respectively. Title pages will be prepared in manuscript.

WAR DIARY
or
INTELLIGENCE SUMMARY.
(Erase heading not required.)

9 D Am Col
Vol 28

Army Form C. 2118.

Place	Date	Hour	Summary of Events and Information	Remarks and references to Appendices
NURLU	1.2.18 to 4.2.18		Column camped at NURLU. Engaged on Fatigues & Erecting Huts and Stables etc	
	4.2.18		Column moved to BRAY-SUR-SOMME Rest AREA by road.	
	5.2.18 to 28.2.18		Troops billeted in Huts, horses in open. Column undergoing training	

[illegible]

[illegible] Capt.
for Major
[illegible] DIVISIONAL COLUMN

T2134. Wt. W708-776. 500000. 4/15. Sir J. C. & S.

72

73

9th Div.

WAR
DIARY

9th DIVISIONAL AMMUNITION COLUMN, R.F.A.

M A R C H

1 9 1 8

9th DAC

Instructions regarding War Diaries and Intelligence Summaries are contained in F. S. Regs., Part II. and the Staff Manual respectively. Title pages will be prepared in manuscript.

WAR DIARY
or
~~INTELLIGENCE SUMMARY.~~
(*Erase heading not required.*)

Army Form C. 2118.

9 D Am Col
Vol 29

Place	Date	Hour	Summary of Events and Information	Remarks and references to Appendices
HAUT ALLAINES	1/3/18		Column marched to HAUT ALLAINES and bivouaced.	
ST RADEGONDE	4/3/18		Column moved to ST RADEGONDE (near PERONNE) and bivouaced.	
MOISLAINS	13/3/18		Column marched up to MOISLAINS and encamped. Up to and including the 21st inst Column was engaged on Corps fatigues and supplying ammunition to Battery positions also dumping a certain amount of Ammunition at reserve Battery positions ready for any emergency.	
	21/3/18		German offensive commenced	
	22/3/18		Column marched to COMBLES after having dumped ammunition at GREEN LINE running N. + S. through MOISLAINS. SAA Section marched to BOUCHAVESNES to work with the Infantry and rejoined main body of Unit on the morning of the 23rd.	
	23/3/18		Column marched to MONTAUBAN; SAA Sec proceeding to LE PLATEAU and remained there for the night.	
	24/3/18		Column marched to GROVETOWN and encamped. Position taken up was within a few yards of the position occupied by the Column during the first Battle of the Somme July 1. 1916.	
	25/3/18		Column marched to MERICOURT L'ABBÉ. On arrival there the SAA Section	

T2134. Wt. W708–776. 500000. 4/15. Sir J. C. & S.

74

Instructions regarding War Diaries and Intelligence Summaries are contained in F. S. Regs., Part II. and the Staff Manual respectively. Title pages will be prepared in manuscript.

Continued.

WAR DIARY
or
~~INTELLIGENCE SUMMARY.~~
(Erase heading not required.)

Army Form C. 2118.

Place	Date	Hour	Summary of Events and Information	Remarks and references to Appendices
			returned to FRICOURT ~~[illegible]~~ to pick up dismounted cavalry and transport them to VILLE-SUR-ANCRE.	
	26/3/18		Column marched to WARLOY and encamped for the night. Ammunition was supplied to Unit during the night by lorry.	
	27/3/18		Column marched to TOUTENCOURT and encamped remaining there till 31/3/18. During the whole of the retirement the Column supplied the Battery wagon lines with ammunition and when possible dumped any ammunition available at any know future Battery positions. Officers men, animals, wagons etc were posted and handed over to Batteries to replace casualties and deficiencies	
			R. S. Perry Capt RHA Commanding 9th D.A.C. RHA.	

75

97

9th Divisional Artillery.

9th DIVISIONAL AMMUNITION COLUMN R.F.A.

APRIL 1918.

9th D. A. C.

Instructions regarding War Diaries and Intelligence Summaries are contained in F. S. Regs., Part I. and the Staff Manual respectively. Title pages will be prepared in manuscript.

WAR DIARY
or
INTELLIGENCE SUMMARY.
(Erase heading not required.)

Army Form C. 2118.

HEADQUARTERS 30/4/18 DIVISIONAL

Vol 30

98

Place	Date	Hour	Summary of Events and Information	Remarks and references to Appendices
TOUTENCOURT	1/4/18		Unit at TOUTENCOURT. No 2 & SAA Sec left for BOURDON en route for HANGEST to entrain.	
	2/4/18		Headqrs and No1 Sec left TOUTENCOURT for AMIENS where they entrained.	
LOCRE	3/4/18		Headqrs No 1 + 2 Sections after detraining at HOPOUTRE arrived at LOCRE. SAA Sec. proceeded to DAYLIGHT CORNER.	
WESTOUTRE	11/4/18		Column marched to WESTOUTRE and encamped just WEST of village.	
POPERINGHE	15/4/18		Column moved to camp S.S.W of POPERINGHE and encamped.	
	18/4/18		Column moved to camp near HOOGRAAF and encamped.	
	25/4/18		Column moved to camp at L.16.b.8.2 (Sheet 27) and remained there for the remainder of the month. On 29/4/18 the SAA Section marched to WINNEZEELE to be near the Infantry for duty. From the 9th inst Nos 1 + 2 sections were continuously engaged in assisting Batteries transporting ammunition to Gun line and Wagon lines, the SAA Sec being engaged on work for the Infantry.	

R G Perry Capt. R.F.A.
O.C. 9th Divisional Column

T2134. Wt. W708-776. 500000. 4/15. Sir J. C. & S.

9th D.A.C.

Army Form C. 2118.

Instructions regarding War Diaries and Intelligence Summaries are contained in F. S. Regs., Part II. and the Staff Manual respectively. Title Pages will be prepared in manuscript.

WAR DIARY
~~or~~
~~INTELLIGENCE SUMMARY~~

(Erase heading not required.)

HEADQUARTERS 9th DIVISIONAL COLUMN No. Date 31/5/18

Vol 31

Place	Date	Hour	Summary of Events and Information	Remarks and references to Appendices
POPERINGHE	1-5-18 to 13.5.18		Headqrs, Nos 1 & 2 Sections of Column encamped, and were engaged in carrying Ammunition to Batteries and Battery Wagon Lines. S.A.A Sec encamped at WINNEZEELE being detached from Unit with the Div. Infantry. On May 3rd S.A.A. Sec moved to PITGAM T.22 a. 4 5 (Sheet 19) and remained there until 6/5/18 moving to LEDERZEELE, encamped for the night, and, moved to RACQUINGHEM on 7/5/18 and encamped.	
WINNEZEELE	13.5-18 to 17.5-18		Headqrs, Nos 1 & 2 Sections marched to WINNEZEELE and occupied Billets and camps.	
RACQUINGHEM	17-5-18 to 26.5.18		Headqrs, Nos 1 & 2 Sections marched to RACQUINGHEM and encamped. The whole of the Column being together again.	
EECKE	26-5-18 to 31.5-18		Headqrs, Nos 1 & 2 Sections marched to EECKE area and occupied camps on 26/5/18. SAA Sec marched to, and encamped at U.12. a (Sheet 27) working with the Infantry. Ammunition Refilling point taken over at Q 19 b. (Sheet 27) and Ammunition supplied to Batteries from this point.	

[signature]
Major R.F.A.
O.C. 9th DIVISIONAL COLUMN

100

2449 Wt. W14957/M90 750,000 1/16 J.B.C. & A. Forms/C.2118/12.

9. D.A.C.

Instructions regarding War Diaries and Intelligence Summaries are contained in F. S. Regs., Part II. and the Staff Manual respectively. Title pages will be prepared in manuscript.

WAR DIARY
~~or~~
~~INTELLIGENCE~~ SUMMARY.
(Erase heading not required.)

Army Form C. 2118.

HEADQUARTERS No. .... Date 30/6/18 9th DIVISIONAL COLUMN

Vol 32

Place	Date	Hour	Summary of Events and Information	Remarks and references to Appendices
EECKE	1/6/18 to 30/6/18		Headqrs, No 1 & 2 Sections at EECKE. Engaged during the month in supplying ammunition to Batteries, Clearing up empties and abandoned ammunition in the Div. Area.	
			S.A.A. Sec at U.12.a (Sheet 27) engaged on salvage work and supplying the Infantry with S.A.A, Bombs etc.	
	17/6/18		Reduction in Establishment of 36 Drivers and 72 animals leaving all gun Ammunition wagons 4 horse teams.	

[illegible] Capt
~~[illegible]~~ Major, R.F.A
O.C. 9th DIVISIONAL COLUMN

T2134. Wt. W708-776. 500000. 4/15. Sir J. C. & S.

9th D.A.C.

Instructions regarding War Diaries and Intelligence Summaries are contained in F. S. Regs., Part II. and the Staff Manual respectively. Title Pages will be prepared in manuscript.

WAR DIARY
or
~~INTELLIGENCE SUMMARY~~

(Erase heading not required.)

Army Form C. 2118.

HEADQUARTERS No. ...... Date 31-7-18 9th DIVISIONAL COLUMN

Vol 33

Place	Date	Hour	Summary of Events and Information	Remarks and references to Appendices
EECKE	1/7/18 to 21/7/18		Headqrs Nos 1 + 2 Sections encamped at EECKE.	
	22-7-18		Headqrs Nos 1 + 2 Sections marched to camp at approximately P.36. central Sheet 27. Engaged during the whole of the month in supplying ammunition to Batteries as required	
			S.A.A. Section remained encamped at V.12.a.4.5 (Sheet 27) for the whole of the month and were engaged on various fatigues, salvage, R.E. work, etc and supplying the Infantry with bombs, ammunition etc.	

for [signature] Capt
~~LIEUT.-COL.~~, R.F.A.
O.C. 9th DIVISIONAL COLUMN

2449 Wt. W14957/M90 750,000 1/16 J.B.C. & A. Forms/C.2118/12.

102

9th D.A.C.

Instructions regarding War Diaries and Intelligence Summaries are contained in F. S. Regs., Part II. and the Staff Manual respectively. Title Pages will be prepared in manuscript.

WAR DIARY
or
INTELLIGENCE SUMMARY
(Erase heading not required.)

Army Form C. 2118.

HEADQUARTERS No. .... Date 31/8/18 9th DIVISIONAL COLUMN

VR 34

Place	Date	Hour	Summary of Events and Information	Remarks and references to Appendices
ST. SYLVESTRE CAPPEL	1-8-18 to 30-8-18		Headqrs Nos 1 + 2 Sections of the Column remained encamped at P.36.a. Sheet 27. Engaged in supplying ammunition to Batteries.	
V.12.a. (Sheet 27)	1-8-18 to 23-8-18.		SAA Section encamped at V.12.a (Sheet 27) working for the Infantry. About 10 wagons working daily on Harvesting work.	
FLETRE (near)	31-8-18		Headqrs Nos 1 + 2 Sections moved forward to W.4.b (Sheet 27) approximately, and commenced salving ammunition from vacated Battery positions.	
WARDRECQUES area	24-8-18 to 31-8-18.		SAA Sec moved out to the WARDRECQUES area with the Infantry the latter having been relieved in the Line on 24th inst.	

for [signature] Capt
~~LIEUT.-COL.~~, R.F.A.
C.C. 9th DIVISIONAL COLUMN

2449 Wt. W14957/M90 750,000 1/16 J.B.C. & A. Forms/C.2118/12.

103

9 D. Am Col

Army Form C. 2118.

Instructions regarding War Diaries and Intelligence Summaries are contained in F. S. Regs., Part II. and the Staff Manual respectively. Title Pages will be prepared in manuscript.

WAR DIARY

or

~~INTELLIGENCE SUMMARY~~

(Erase heading not required.)

HEADQUARTERS No. ...... Date 30/9/18 9th DIVISIONAL COLUMN

Vol 35

Place	Date	Hour	Summary of Events and Information	Remarks and references to Appendices
ST SYLVESTRE CAPPEL	21/8/18		Headqrs No 1 & 2 Sections encamped. SAA Section near WARDRECQUES with the Infantry.	
CAESTRE (near)	1-9-18 to 12.9.18		Headqrs Nos 1 & 2 Sections moved to the area between CAESTRE and FLETRE on 1-9-18 and whilst there were engaged in salving ammunition, camouflage etc from vacated Battery positions.	
HAANDEKOT AREA	12.9.18 27.9.18		Headqrs Nos 1 & 2 Sections marched to the HAANDEKOT area (near PROVEN) and occupied Camps. SAA Section moved to the WORMHOUDT area with the Infantry on 12.9.18. On 20/9/18 No 2 Sec moved up to the HAMHOEK area to work with 51st Bde RFA.	
HAMHOEK AREA	Night of 27/28/9/18		Headqrs and No 1 Sec moved up to HAMHOEK AREA	
VLAMERTINGHE	28/9/18		Headqrs, Nos 1 & 2 Sections moved up to EAST of VLAMERTINGHE. SAA Section also moved up to VLAMERTINGHE area.	
YPRES	29/9/18		SAA Section moved to the EAST of YPRES	
—	30/9/18		Headqrs, Nos 1 & 2 Sections moved to the EAST of YPRES. Ammunition taken up to ZONNEBEKE Area and EAST of it. Roads very congested with traffic and engagement from 14 to 18 hours at a time	

105

G Duff Major
~~Lieut.~~ R.F.A.
O.C. 9th DIVISIONAL COLUMN

2449 Wt. W14957/M90 750,000 1/16 J.B.C. &

Instructions regarding War Diaries and Intelligence Summaries are contained in F. S. Regs., Part II. and the Staff Manual respectively. Title Pages will be prepared in manuscript.

WAR DIARY
or
INTELLIGENCE SUMMARY
(Erase heading not required.)

Army Form C. 2118.

HEADQUARTERS 9th DIVISIONAL COLUMN No. Date 31.10.18.

Vol 36

106

Place	Date	Hour	Summary of Events and Information	Remarks and references to Appendices
POTIJZE	1/10/18 to 14/10/18		Unit encamped in POTIJZE area.	
KEIBERG } SLYPSCAPPEL	14.10.18		Unit moved to KEIBERG during the morning and moved forward to SLYPSCAPPEL during the afternoon.	
ROLLEGHEMCAPPELE	15/10/18 to 20/10/18		Unit moved to ROLLEGHEM-CAPPELLE and encamped remaining there until 20.10.18.	
	17.10.18		SAA section moved to vicinity of WINKEL-ST.ELOI.	
ST CATHERINE CAPPELLE	20/10/18 to 22/10/18		Headqrs, No 1 + 2 Sections moved to vicinity of ST CATHERINE-CAPPELLE.	
			SAA section moved to STOKERIJ area.	
STOKERIJ	22/10/18 to 25/10/18		Headqrs, No 1 + 2 Sections moved to STOKERIJ.	
			SAA section moved to BAVICHOVE	
HARLEBEKE	25.10.18.		Headqrs No 1, 2 and SAA sections moved to the vicinity of HARLEBEKE.	
	29.10.18		SAA section marched to G 12 c Sheet 29	
	31.10.18		Headqrs, No 1 + 2 Sections marched to G 12 c Sheet 29.	
			During the whole of the period under review Column engaged on Ammunition duties. Forward Dumps were established within easy reach of Battery wagon Lines and vacated Battery positions cleared forward to these Dumps in addition to supplying Batteries with ammunition, or dumping it at convenient points.	
			SAA Section worked for the Infantry only and at each step of the advance established a forward Echelon.	

for [signature] Capt. ~~LT. COL.~~, R.F.A.
Comdg. 9th DIVISIONAL COLUMN

2449 Wt. W14957/M90 750,000 1/16 J.B.C. & A. Forms/C.2118/12.

Army Form C. 2118.

Instructions regarding War Diaries and Intelligence Summaries are contained in F. S. Regs., Part II. and the Staff Manual respectively. Title Pages will be prepared in manuscript.

WAR DIARY
or
~~INTELLIGENCE SUMMARY~~

(Erase heading not required.)

HEADQUARTERS 9th DIVISIONAL COLUMN
No. ......
Date 30/11/18.

VIII 37

Place	Date	Hour	Summary of Events and Information	Remarks and references to Appendices
HUELE	1/11/18 to 13/11/18.		Column encamped at HUELE in Rest Billets.	
VICHTE	14/11/18		Column marched to the VICHTE area and encamped. This march constituted the first of a series of marches towards the RHINE.	
RENAIX	15/11/18		Column marched to RENAIX.	
NEDERBRAKEL	18/11/18		Column marched to NEDERBRAKEL.	
TENBOSCH	20/11/18		Column marched to TENBOSCH.	
NEYGHEM	21/11/18		Column marched to NEYGHEM	
TOURNEPPE	23/11/18		Column marched to TOURNEPPE.	
BIERGES	25/11/18		Column marched to BIERGES	
HUPPAYE	27/11/18		Column marched to HUPPAYE.	
MOXHE	28/11/18		Column marched to MOXHE.	
AMPSIN	29/11/18		Column marched to AMPSIN and remained there on the 30th inst.	
			During the whole of the above marches there were no casualties to animals.	

for [signature] Capt
~~Lieut-Col.~~ R.F.A.
C.C. 9th DIVISIONAL COLUMN

2449 Wt. W14957/M90 750,000 1/16 J.B.C. & A. Forms/C.2118/12.

[o]

Instructions regarding War Diaries and Intelligence Summaries are contained in F. S. Regs., Part II. and the Staff Manual respectively. Title Pages will be prepared in manuscript.

WAR DIARY

~~or~~

~~INTELLIGENCE SUMMARY~~

(Erase heading not required.)

Army Form C. 2118.

HEADQUARTERS 9th DIVISIONAL COLUMN No. 31/12/18

9 D Am Col

Vol 38

Place	Date	Hour	Summary of Events and Information	Remarks and references to Appendices
VAUX-SUR-CHEVREMONT	1/12/18 to 4/12/18		Column in billets at VAUX-SUR-CHEVREMONT.	
VERVIERS	4/12/18		Column marched to VERVIERS.	
EUPEN	5/12/18		Column marched to the EUPEN area.	
MERODE	6/12/18		Column marched to the MERODE area	
KERPEN	7/12/18.		Column marched to the KERPEN area	
BOCKLEMUND	8/12/18.		Column marched to the area of BUCKLEMUND Headqrs just south of the village.	
STAMMHEIM	13/12/18		Column marched through COLOGNE and across the RIVER RHINE through MULHEIM to STAMMHEIM.	
LANGENFELD	15/12/18		Column marched to the LANGENFELD area. Headqrs and SAA Section at LANGENFELD No 1 Section at RICHRATH and No 2 Section at IMMIGRATH. All three villages were in 9th Div. Rub area host.	
OHLIGS	21/12/18		Column moved to the OHLIGS area. Headquarters north of the village, Nos 1 & 2 Sections in OHLIGS. SAA Section south of the village but moved to HILDEN.	

[signature] Major, R.F.A.
O.C. 9th DIVISIONAL COLUMN

2449 Wt. W14957/M90 750,000 1/16 J.B.C. & A. Forms/C.2118/12.

9th DAC

Instructions regarding War Diaries and Intelligence Summaries are contained in F. S. Regs., Part II. and the Staff Manual respectively. Title pages will be prepared in manuscript.

WAR DIARY

or

~~INTELLIGENCE SUMMARY.~~

(*Erase heading not required.*)

1439

CHECK

Army Form C. 2118.

9 D 39

Hour, Date, Place	Summary of Events and Information	Remarks and references to Appendices
January 1 - 31/1919	Column remained in Billets as for December 1918. Headquarters at the SCHLOSS CASTERBROICH. No1 + 2 Sections at OHLIGS and SAA Section at HILDEN.	u.e

G. Dull
Major R.F.A.
Commanding 9th D.A.C.

(73989) W4141—463. 400,000. 9/14. H.&J.Ltd. Forms/C. 2118/10.

Army Form C. 2118.

110

Instructions regarding War Diaries and Intelligence Summaries are contained in F. S. Regs., Part II and the Staff Manual respectively. Title Pages will be prepared in manuscript.

INTELLIGENCE SUMMARY

(Erase heading not required.)

Vol 40

Place	Date	Hour	Summary of Events and Information	Remarks and references to Appendices
Feby 1st to 28th/1919.			Column remained in Billets as for January 1919. i.e., Headquarters at the SCHLOSS CASPERBROICH. Nos 1+2 Sections at OHLIGS. and S.A.A. Section at HILDEN.	

HEADQUARTERS
No. ....
Date ....
9th DIVISIONAL COLUMN

[illegible] Major R.F.A.
Commanding 9th D.A.C.

D.A.C.

Instructions regarding War Diaries and Intelligence Summaries are contained in F. S. Regs., Part II. and the Staff Manual respectively. Title Pages will be prepared in manuscript.

WAR DIARY
or
INTELLIGENCE SUMMARY
(Erase heading not required.)

Army Form C. 2118.

Vol 41

Place	Date	Hour	Summary of Events and Information	Remarks and references to Appendices
March 1st to 31st/1919.			Column remained in Billets as for February 1919. i.e.,	
			Headqrs at the SCHLOSS CASPERBROICH.	
			Nos 1 + 2 Sections at OHLIGS.	
			S.A.A. Section at HILDEN.	
			[signature] Major R.F.A. Commanding. Lowland. Div. Column	
			31. 3. 19.	

111

2449 Wt. W14957/M90 750,000 1/16 J.B.C. & A. Forms/C.2118/12.

Instructions regarding War Diaries and Intelligence Summaries are contained in F. S. Regs., Part II. and the Staff Manual respectively. Title Pages will be prepared in manuscript.

LOWLAND D.A.C.

WAR DIARY
or
INTELLIGENCE SUMMARY
(Erase heading not required.)

Army Form C. 2118.

Vol 42

Place	Date	Hour	Summary of Events and Information	Remarks and references to Appendices
April 1st to 30th			Headqrs, No 2 + S.A.A. Sections remained in billets as for March 1919. i.e.,	
			Headqrs at the SCHLOSS CASPERSBROICH	
			No 2 Section at OHLIGS.	
			S.A.A. Section at HILDEN	
			No 1 Section moved as follows:-	
April 28th			From OHLIGS to WALD (Taking over Transport Lines + accommodation vacated by 5/6 Royal Scots.)	

HEADQUARTERS LOWLAND DIVISIONAL AMMUNITION COLUMN

R A Bendle
MAJOR R. F. A.
COMMANDING LOWLAND DIVISIONAL COLUMN.

112

Lowland. D.A.C.

Army Form C. 2118

Instructions regarding War Diaries and Intelligence Summaries are contained in F. S. Regs., Part II. and the Staff Manual respectively. Title Pages will be prepared in manuscript.

WAR DIARY
or
INTELLIGENCE SUMMARY
(Erase heading not required.)

Place	Date	Hour	Summary of Events and Information	Remarks and references to Appendices
May 1st	to 31st		Headquarters, No 2 & S.A.A. Sections remained in billets as for April 1919 i.e.,	
			Headquarters at the SCHLOSS CASPERSBROICH.	
			No 2 Section at OHLIGS	
			S.A.A. Section at HILDEN	
			No 1 Section moved as follows:-	
May 2nd			From WALD to MERSHEID (taking over Billet vacated by "A" 51st BATTERY)	

HEADQUARTERS LOWLAND DIVISIONAL AMMUNITION COLUMN

R A Beadle
MAJOR R.F.A.
COMMANDING LOWLAND DIVISIONAL COLUMN.

113

2449 Wt. W14957/M90 750,000 1/16 J.B.C. & A. Forms/C.2118/12.

LOWLAND. D.A.C.

Instructions regarding War Diaries and Intelligence Summaries are contained in F. S. Regs., Part II. and the Staff Manual respectively. Title Pages will be prĕpared in manuscript.

WAR DIARY
or
INTELLIGENCE SUMMARY
(Erase heading not required.)

Army Form C. 2118.

Place	Date	Hour	Summary of Events and Information	Remarks and references to Appendices
Ohligs Germany	1/6/19 to 30/6/19		Headquarters of Column at SCHLOSS CASPERSBROICH. No 1 Section at MERSCHIED. No 2 Section at OHLIGS and the SAA Section at HILDEN. The Unit was prepared to march into Germany on 23/6/19 should this have been necessary. A. Townsend. Capt RHA Commanding Lowland D.A.C.	

Lowland D.A.C.

Instructions regarding War Diaries and Intelligence Summaries are contained in F. S. Regs., Part II. and the Staff Manual respectively. Title Pages will be prepared in manuscript.

WAR DIARY
or
INTELLIGENCE SUMMARY
(Erase heading not required.)

Army Form C. 2118.

Place	Date	Hour	Summary of Events and Information	Remarks and references to Appendices
OHLIGS	1.7.19		Headquarters at SCHLOSS CASPERSBROICH. No 1 Section at MERSCHEID. No 2 Section at OHLIGS and S.A.A. Section at HILDEN.	
	11.7.19		Column left Billets in OHLIGS Area and marched to COLOGNE - MULHEIM.	
	12.7.19.		Column marched to Area of POULHEIM.	
	13.7.19.		Column marched to the Area of OBEREMPT - KIRCHTROISDORF. Headqrs and No 1 Section billetted at KIRCHTROISDORF. No 2 and S.A.A. Section billetted at OBEREMPT.	
			H. S. Pennington Lieut for Major R.F.A. Commanding Lowland D.A.C.	
			2.8.19.	

2449 Wt. W14957/M90 750,000 1/16 J.B.C. & A. Forms/C.2118/12.

115

Appendix No/ CCLXXXI

Army Form C. 2118.

WAR DIARY
or
INTELLIGENCE SUMMARY
(Erase heading not required.)

Instructions regarding War Diaries and Intelligence Summaries are contained in F. S. Regs., Part II. and the Staff Manual respectively. Title Pages will be prepared in manuscript.

Place	Date	Hour	Summary of Events and Information	Remarks and references to Appendices
KIRCHTROISDORF	1.8.19		Headquarters and No 1 Section in billets at KIRCHTROISDORF.	
			No 2 + S.A.A. Sections in billets at OBEREMBT.	
			31. 8. 19. L. P. [signature] Capt for Major R.F.A. Commanding. Lowland. D.A.C.	

HEADQUARTERS LOWLAND DIVISIONAL AMMUNITION COLUMN

2449 Wt. W14957/M90 750,000 1/16 J.B.C. & A. Forms/C.2118/12.

1/6

Army Form C. 2118.

APPENDIX No CCLXXXI

Instructions regarding War Diaries and Intelligence Summaries are contained in F. S. Regs., Part II. and the Staff Manual respectively. Title Pages will be prepared in manuscript.

WAR DIARY

~~or~~

~~INTELLIGENCE~~ SUMMARY

(Erase heading not required.)

Place	Date	Hour	Summary of Events and Information	Remarks and references to Appendices
KIRCHTROISDORF	1.9.19		Headquarters and No1 Section in billets at KIRCHTROISDORF.	
			No 2 and S.A.A. Sections at OBEREMBT.	
ELSDORF	29.9.19		Headquarters and No1 Section moved to ELSDORF.	

L. P. Daniell Capt for
Major R.F.A.
Commanding Lowland D.A.C.

9TH DIVISION

9TH DIVL TRENCH MORTAR BTTS.

JLY 1916 - ~~DEC 1918.~~ 1919 JAN

9th Divisional Artillery

9th DIVL. TRENCH MORTAR BATTERIES,

J U L Y, 1 9 1 6.

July

D.W. T M Batteries

9 / Vol I

9th

Head Quarters.

9th. Division.

Reference your 16/77 dated 23/8/16, herewith War Diary for T.M. Brigade for July.

Captain.

2/9/16.

Staff Captain 9th. D. A.

Army Form C. 2118

Instructions regarding War Diaries and Intelligence Summaries are contained in F. S. Regs., Part II. and the Staff Manual respectively. Title Pages will be prepared in manuscript.

WAR DIARY

or

~~INTELLIGENCE SUMMARY~~

(Erase heading not required.)

Place	Date	Hour	Summary of Events and Information	Remarks and references to Appendices
Somme.	1st July	7.30 AM.	Attack on Montauban Sector by 18th Div'n and 30th Div'n. This unit was in support of 18th Div'n. T.M. Btys. Followed up the attack and reconnoitred for positions for defensive work in the event of a counter attack. Noticed that all wire had been thoroughly cut, and afforded little obstacle. Selected 6 positions covering our front line and commenced preparing same. Arranged forward bomb store and supply of ammunition.	
	2nd "		Continued work on forward emplacements.	
	3rd "		Do. Do.	
	4th "		Guns in position with 20 rounds of ammunition. Used hand-carts to take same up which proved of great value.	
	5th "		No Change.	
	6th "		" "	
	12th "		All guns and personell returned to Hdqrs and placed at disposal of B.G.R.A. who used same as reinforcements for Field Batteries.	
	13th "			
Longueval.	14th "		Followed up 9th Div'n Infantry attack on Longueval for reconnaisance purposes. Was heavily shelled by "tear" shells which appear to be fired from a quick firer or "pom-pom".	

1875 Wt. W593/826 1,000,000 4/15 J.B.C. & A. A.D.S.S./Forms/C. 2118.

Army Form C. 2118

Instructions regarding War Diaries and Intelligence Summaries are contained in F. S. Regs., Part II. and the Staff Manual respectively. Title Pages will be prepared in manuscript.

WAR DIARY
or
~~INTELLIGENCE SUMMARY~~
(Erase heading not required.)

Place	Date	Hour	Summary of Events and Information	Remarks and references to Appendices
Longueval.	14th July	8 P.M.	Received instructions from H.Q.R.A. to report to F.O.O. 52nd Bde. R.F.A. at Longueval. Took 2 Officers and 12 men with 2 guns complete, and arranged for Infantry carrying party to bring up 50 rounds 2". Lack of transport was very noticeable, and men were quite fatigued at the end of the journey. Very difficult to find him, and when I was successful in my efforts, he could give me no information. Reported to O.C. Black Watch who did not require my services, so established Hdqrs on border of Longueval, and returned to R.A. for orders.	
	15th "	8 P.M.	Battery in action on enemy strong points, which were holding up Infantry. Am of the opinion that "strong points" are "mobile" machine guns, being very cleverly moved from one place to another. Engaged houses in main street of village, and set 3 on fire. Lack of delay action fuzes noticeable. Observation good and telephone communication excellent, owing to small amount of wire necessary from O.P. to Battery. The guns proved very mobile, and were quickly got into action.	
	16th "	10 a.m.	Opened fire on houses and ejected 5 of the enemy who were immediately sniped. The 2" Mortar is a great asset in street fighting, but delay action fuzes are necessary, as we are using "direct action" which immediately detonate, when coming in contact with the roof of buildings. Notice that snipers are quiet when mortars	

1875 Wt. W593/826 1,000,000 4/15 J.B.C. & A. A.D.S.S./Forms/C. 2118.

Instructions regarding War Diaries and Intelligence Summaries are contained in F. S. Regs., Part II. and the Staff Manual respectively. Title Pages will be prepared in manuscript.

WAR DIARY
or
INTELLIGENCE SUMMARY
(Erase heading not required.)

Army Form C. 2118.

Place	Date	Hour	Summary of Events and Information	Remarks and references to Appendices
Longueval.	16th July	10 a.m.	are in action. Doubtless they go to earth.	
		4.15 p.m.	Instructed to demolish a redoubt, but observation is impossible. Ammunition replenished by Infantry carrying parties.	
	17 "	9 a.m.	Ready to commence on all day bombardment, but was stopped by Infantry as patrols were reconnoitring. Later, withdrew to Hdqrs as our Artillery were heavily bombarding village.	
	18 "		Reconnoitred a position in Delville Wood for wire cutting purposes. Foliage was then too thick to enable me to ~~find~~ fire, and the task was entrusted to 6 inch. 2 O.R. were killed on this day.	
	19th "		As a new line was run through the centre of the village, an Officer was sent to reconnoitre Battery position, but no available place could be found.	
	20th "		Ordered by O.C. 10th Suffolks. 18th Div'n. to withdraw my guns.	
	21st "		Took over a 240 m.m. French Mortar. Reconnoitred emplacement in old German Trench running on border of Longueval. Took up gun in the evening by G.S. wagon, and also 30 rounds of ammunition.	
	22nd "		240 m.m. T.M. ready for action, but orders were received not to fire.	

1875 Wt. W593/825 1,000,000 4/15 J.B.C. & A. A.D.S.S./Forms/C. 2118.

Instructions regarding War Diaries and Intelligence Summaries are contained in F. S. Regs., Part II. and the Staff Manual respectively. Title Pages will be prepared in manuscript.

WAR DIARY
or
~~INTELLIGENCE SUMMARY~~
(Erase heading not required.)

Army Form C. 2118

Place	Date	Hour	Summary of Events and Information	Remarks and references to Appendices
Longueval.	23rd July		Participated in preliminary bombardment, firing 4 rounds on hostile barrier. 6 rounds were fired at various "strong points" during the day. 1 Officer wounded. Little retaliation on the emplacement.	
	24th "		4 rounds fired during hostile counter attack.	
	25th "		Fired one round but was stopped firing further by O.C. 12th Gloucesters, as hostile retaliation had buried one of their machine guns.	
	26th "	8 A.M.	Fired 4 rounds and reconnoitred for position of second 240 m.m.	
			Positions taken over by 2nd Divn.	
	27th "		Removed Hdqrs to Grovetown.	
	28th "		" " " Vaux-sur-Somme.	
	29th "		Resting at Vaux-sur-Somme.	
	30th "		" " " "	
	31st "		Entrained in Motor Lorries for 1st Army area.	

J. S. Laidman Capt. RA.
Comdg. 9th T. M. Brigade.

1/9/16.

1875 Wt. W593/826 1,000,000 4/15 J.B.C. & A. A.D.S.S./Forms/C. 2118.

9th Divisional Artillery.

27th TRENCH MORTAR BATTERY,

J U L Y, 1 9 1 6.

9

July

Army Form C. 2118.

27th Trench Mortar Battery

Vol 1

WAR DIARY
or
INTELLIGENCE SUMMARY

(Erase heading not required.)

Instructions regarding War Diaries and Intelligence Summaries are contained in F. S. Regs., Part II. and the Staff Manual respectively. Title Pages will be prepared in manuscript.

Place	Date	Hour	Summary of Events and Information	Remarks and references to Appendices
BILLON VALLEY	1.7.16 2.7.16		The Battery was in dug-outs in BILLON VALLEY	Ref Sheets 62D NE 62C NW 1/20,000
		7 pm	The Battery commenced to relieve the 90th Battery in MONTAUBAN. Owing to congestion in SUPPORT AVENUE the relief was not completed until	
MONTAUBAN	3.7.16		5 AM. By 12 noon six Guns were in position of defence as follows:- 2 Guns in F. KEEP 2 guns in "A" KEEP in MONTAUBAN + 2 guns in TRAIN ALLEY. 100 Rounds were with each gun + a central dump was established in SOUTH TRENCH. Ammunition was brought up to this dump by a carrying party furnished by Bde.	MONTAUBAN MAP 1/20,000
		9.PM.	3 Guns were sent forward after the Infantry had reached their Objective viz BERNAFAY WOOD. They took up positions in SE corner of wood NE corner of wood + MONTAUBAN ALLEY respectively. 50 rounds went forward with each gun.	
MONTAUBAN + BERNAFAY WOOD	4.7.16	6 pm	Positions of guns at this stage were:- 2 guns in F KEEP, MONTAUBAN. 2 guns in MONTAUBAN ALLEY at S22 d 9.1. 2 in newly dug trench at S28 b 2.5. 1 gun at S29 C4.6. + one gun in reserve in TRAIN ALLEY. Central Dump changed from SOUTH TRENCH to TRAIN ALLEY	
	5.7.16 6.7.16 7.7.16		No change in situation. Shelling continuously sustained by the enemy.	

2449 Wt. W14957/M90 750,000 1/16 J.B.C. & A. Forms/C.2118/12.

Instructions regarding War Diaries and Intelligence Summaries are contained in F. S. Regs., Part II. and the Staff Manual respectively. Title Pages will be prepared in manuscript.

WAR DIARY
or
INTELLIGENCE SUMMARY
(Erase heading not required.)

Army Form C. 2118.

Place	Date	Hour	Summary of Events and Information	Remarks and references to Appendices
BILLON VALLEY	8.7.16	3pm	The Battery, the Brigade being relieved, went into rest in Dug outs in BILLON VALLEY	
	9.7.16 10.7.16 11.7.16 12.7.16 13.7.16		The Battery was resting & refitting.	
LONGUEVAL		6pm	The Battery left BILLON VALLEY & proceeded to TALUS BOISE being accompanied by 50 men	
		11pm	of the KOSB who were attached as carrying party. At TALUS BOISE 2 guns joined the 11th Royal Scots 2 guns joined the 12th Royal Scots & 2 guns joined the 9th Scottish Rifles 50 rounds were carried with each gun.	
	14.7.16		Three guns went forward with the 3rd wave of each Battn to the assault of the enemy line at LONGUEVAL. The remaining two guns were kept in reserve in CATERPILLAR VALLEY. When the line had been captured ~~the~~ guns were placed in defensive positions as follows:- one gun at S16d9.0 One at S17a3.4 2 at S17a9.4 & one at S17a7.2, one gun having been knocked out of action. 100 rounds were with each gun and a central dump established at S17a2.2.	MONTAUBAN MAP 1/20000
	15.7.16 16.7.16 17.7.16 18.7.16 19.7.16		4 guns were centred at S17.a9.4 to shoot on strong point at S17b3.8. When this shoot was finished only one gun was left in action, two going out with loose collars & one with a broken collar. Defensive positions were then as follows 1 gun at S17a9.4 1 at S17a3.4 & 2 at S17a7.2. One of the two at S17a7.2 was subsequently put out of action.	
TALUS BOISE	20.7.16	5am	The Battery was relieved & proceeded to TALUS BOISE	
CITADEL		4.30pm	Marched to CITADEL	

Army Form C. 2118.

Instructions regarding War Diaries and Intelligence Summaries are contained in F. S. Regs., Part II. and the Staff Manual respectively. Title Pages will be prepared in manuscript.

WAR DIARY
or
INTELLIGENCE SUMMARY
(Erase heading not required.)

Place	Date	Hour	Summary of Events and Information	Remarks and references to Appendices
CITADEL	21.7.16		} Resting	
	22.7.16			
MERICOURT L'ABEE	23.7.16		Marched to MERICOURT L'ABEE where the Battery entrained for HANGEST	AMIENS MAP 1/100.000
HANGEST	24.7.16		Marched from HANGEST to billets in BELLANCOURT	ABBEVILLE 1/100000
BELLANCOURT	25.7.16		Entrained at PONT REMY for DIEVAL whence by route march to billets at BRUAY	LENS 1/100000
BRUAY	26.7.16		} Reorganisation + refitting of Battery at BRUAY	
"	27.7.16			
"	28.7.16			
"	29.7.16			
"	30.7.16			
DIEVAL	31.7.16		Marched to DIEVAL.	

R Whyte 2/Lt
Commanding 27th TMB.

2449 Wt. W14957/M90 750,000 1/16 J.B.C. & A. Forms/C.2118/12.

Army Form C. 2118.

Instructions regarding War Diaries and Intelligence Summaries are contained in F. S. Regs., Part II. and the Staff Manual respectively. Title Pages will be prepared in manuscript.

WAR DIARY
or
INTELLIGENCE SUMMARY
(Erase heading not required.)

27th Trench Mortar Battery

Place	Date	Hour	Summary of Events and Information	Remarks and references to Appendices
BILLON VALLEY	1.7.16 2.7.16		The Battery was in dug-outs in BILLON VALLEY	Ref maps 62 D.N.E. 62C NW 1/20000
		7 pm	The Battery commenced to relieve the 90th Battery in MONTAUBAN. Owing to congestion in SUPPORT AVENUE the relief was not completed until 5 AM.	MONTAUBAN MAP 1/20000
MONTAUBAN	3.7.16		By 12 noon the Guns were in position of defence as follows:- 2 Guns in F KEEP 2 guns in 'A' KEEP in MONTAUBAN, + 2 guns in TRAIN ALLEY 100 Rounds were with each gun + a central dump was established in SOUTH TRENCH. Ammunition was brought up to this dump by a carrying party furnished by Bde.	
		9 PM	3 Guns were sent forward after the Infantry had reached their Objective viz BERNAFAY WOOD. They took up positions in SE Corner of Wood NE Corner of Wood + MONTAUBAN ALLEY respectively. 50 rounds went forward with each gun.	
MONTAUBAN + BERNAFAY WOOD.	4.7.16	6 pm	Positions of guns at this stage were:- 2 guns in F. KEEP, MONTAUBAN. 2 guns in MONTAUBAN ALLEY at S22d91. 2 in newly dug trench at S28 b 2.5 1 gun at S29 C46, one gun in reserve in TRAIN ALLEY. Central Dump changed from SOUTH TRENCH to TRAIN ALLEY	
	5.7.16 6.7.16 7.7.16		No change in situation. Shelling continuously sustained by the enemy.	

Army Form C. 2118.

Instructions regarding War Diaries and Intelligence Summaries are contained in F. S. Regs., Part II. and the Staff Manual respectively. Title Pages will be prepared in manuscript.

WAR DIARY
or
INTELLIGENCE SUMMARY

(Erase heading not required.)

Place	Date	Hour	Summary of Events and Information	Remarks and references to Appendices
BILLON VALLEY	8.7.16	3pm	The Battery, the Brigade being relieved, went into rest in Dug outs in BILLON VALLEY	
	9.7.16 10.7.16 11.7.16 12.7.16 13.7.16		The Battery was resting & refitting.	
LONGUEVAL		6pm 11pm	The Battery left BILLON VALLEY & proceeded to TALUS BOISE being accompanied by 50 men of the KOSB who were attached as carrying party. At TALUS BOISE 2 guns joined the 11th Royal Scots 2 guns joined the 12th Royal Scots & 2 guns joined the 9th Scottish Rifles. 50 rounds were carried with each gun.	
	14.7.16		These guns went forward with the 3rd wave of each Battn to the assault of the enemy line at LONGUEVAL. The remaining two guns were kept in reserve in CATERPILLAR VALLEY. When the line had been captured the guns were placed in defensive positions as follows:- one gun at S16d90 One at S17a34 2 at S17a94 & one at S17a72, one gun having been knocked out of action. 100 rounds were with each gun and a central dump established at S17a22.	MONTAUBAN MAP 1/20000
	15.7.16 16.7.16 17.7.16 18.7.16 19.7.16		4 guns were centred at S17a9.4 to shoot on strong point at S17b38. When this shoot was finished only one gun was left in action, three going out with loose collars & one with a broken collar. Defensive positions were then as follows 1 gun at S17a94 1 at S17a34 & 2 at S17a72. One of the two at S17a72 was subsequently put out of action.	
TALUS BOISE	20.7.16	5am	The Battery was relieved & proceeded to TALUS BOISE	
CITADEL		4.30pm	Marched to CITADEL	

Army Form C. 2118.

Instructions regarding War Diaries and Intelligence Summaries are contained in F. S. Regs., Part II. and the Staff Manual respectively. Title Pages will be prepared in manuscript.

WAR DIARY
or
INTELLIGENCE SUMMARY
(Erase heading not required.)

Place	Date	Hour	Summary of Events and Information	Remarks and references to Appendices
CITADEL	21.7.16		} Resting	
	22.7.16			
MERICOURT L'ABEE	23.7.16		Marched to MERICOURT L'ABEE where the Battery entrained for HANGEST	AMIENS MAP 1/100000
HANGEST	24.7.16		Marched from HANGEST to billets in BELLANCOURT.	ABBEVILLE 1/100000
BELLANCOURT	25.7.16		Entrained at PONT REMY for DIEVAL whence by route march to billets at BRUAY	LENS 1/100000
BRUAY	26.7.16			
..	27.7.16		Reorganisation & refitting of Battery at BRUAY	
..	28.7.16			
..	29.7.16			
..	30.7.16			
DIEVAL	31.7.16		Marched to DIEVAL	

R Whyte 2/Lt
Commanding 27th TMB.

2449 Wt. W14957/M90 750,000 1/16 J.B.C. & A. Forms/C.2118/12.

9th Divisional Artillery.

27th TRENCH MORTAR BATTERY,

AUGUST, 1916.

Instructions regarding War Diaries and Intelligence Summaries are contained in F. S. Regs., Part II. and the Staff Manual respectively. Title Pages will be prepared in manuscript.

WAR DIARY
or
INTELLIGENCE SUMMARY
(Erase heading not required.)

Army Form C. 2118.

27th Trench Mortar Battery

Vol II

Place	Date	Hour	Summary of Events and Information	Remarks and references to Appendices
DIEVAL	1.8.16 2.8.16 3.8.16 4.8.16 5.8.16 6.8.16 7.8.16 8.8.16 9.8.16 10.8.16 11.8.16 12.8.16		Battery was at DIÉVAL refitting & training	
VILLERS AUX BOIS		2pm	By Routemarch to VILLERS AUX BOIS where the Battery established its HQ.	
	13.8.16	9pm	Half Battery proceeded to the trenches & took over from (103rd) 37th T.M.B. Enemy very active with	
		11pm	Trench Mortars Relief completed by 11pm Positions of mortars on completion of relief as follows S14 b 7.7 2 guns S8 d 75.35 2 guns S8 c 7.9 1 gun.	
	14.8.16		Enemy quiet. A few Minenwerfer bombs fired, which ceased on our retaliating	
	15.8.16	8.0pm	We fired 30 rounds from each gun (150 rds) at request of 11th RS. The enemy retaliation was heavy, firing a large quantity of heavy Minenwerfer.	
	16.8.16		Enemy very quiet we did not fire	
	17.8.16	4.30pm	Half battery were relieved.	
	18.8.16	2pm	We fired 100 rounds (50 each from Nos 1 & 2 guns) at LOVE'S CRATER & front line to left in retaliation	
		4.30pm	for enemy Minenwerfer fire in the morning. He retaliated with heavy Minenwerfer on left of centre sector, firing at a long interval. We fired 10 rounds at NEW CUT CRATER & hostile fire ceased	
	19.8.16		Enemy quiet. No firing done. Work commenced on New bomb Store. We moved a gun from S8 d 75.35 to S8 d 2.9	
	20.8.16	3pm	We registered No 7 gun on FOOTBALL CRATER	
	21.8.16	5pm	We fired 15 rds from No 4 gun at KENNEDY CRATER. Enemy retaliated very heavily - at 6.30pm we fired	
		6.30pm	50 rds from the same gun in conjunction with 2 in battery. Half battery were relieved at 4.30pm	
	22.8.16	2.0pm	We registered No 7 gun on THE DIMPLE, FOOTBALL CRATER & BROADBRIDGE CRATER & No 6 gun on BROADBRIDGE & MILDREN CRATER	

Instructions regarding War Diaries and Intelligence Summaries are contained in F. S. Regs., Part II. and the Staff Manual respectively. Title Pages will be prepared in manuscript.

WAR DIARY
or
INTELLIGENCE SUMMARY

(Erase heading not required.)

Army Form C. 2118.

27 Trench Mortar Battery

Place	Date	Hour	Summary of Events and Information	Remarks and references to Appendices
VILLERS AU BOIS	23/8/16		Enemy very quiet No firing done	
	24/8/16		No 1 gun registered on sap behind LOVE'S CRATER	
CARENCY SECTOR TRENCHES	25.8.16		We registered Nos 7 + 6 guns on wire between S9c 20.05 + S92. 20.20. from temporary emplacements. We also registered in front of CENTRE + RIGHT PICQUETS. A few rounds were fired at post on	
		4.30pm	FOOTBALL CRATER - Half battery relieved.	
	26.8.16		We retaliated with 20 rounds for enemy Minenwerfer fire on left sector.	
	27.8.16		Enemy very quiet. No firing done	
	28.8.16	12 noon	We registered No 4 gun on sap to KENNEDY CRATER + a hostile point to left of same. Work was commenced on No 3 emplacement at about S14 b 5.9. also on dug out at S14 b 7.7	
	29.8.16		Work continued on bomb store + No 3 emplacement Very quiet No firing	
		4.30pm	Half battery relieved	
	30.8.16		Work continued on bomb store + No 3 emplacement.	
	31.8.16		We ranged on wire opposite Sap B2 Work continued on bomb store + No 3 emplacement.	

E H Sanders Lieut
27 T.M.B.
1/9/16.

2449 Wt. W14957/M90 750,000 1/16 B.C. & A. Forms/C.2118/12.

9th Divisional Artillery

26th TRENCH MORTAR BATTERY,

A U G U S T, 1 9 1 6.

Subject War Diaries.
To 37th Division G.

Reference War Diaries enclosed from V.37. Heavy T.M. Battery and X37. T.M. Btty. The Diaries for Y37 and Z37 will follow as soon as possible.

P. L. Bellew Capt.
D.O.T.M. 37th Div. Arty.
attached 9th Div. T.M. Bgde

12/9/16

SECRET

26th. TRENCH. MORTAR. BATTY. WAR DIARY
or
INTELLIGENCE SUMMARY.
(Erase heading not required.)

Army Form C. 2118.

Vol I

Instructions regarding War Diaries and Intelligence Summaries are contained in F. S. Regs., Part II and the Staff Manual respectively. Title pages will be prepared in manuscript.

Hour, Date, Place	Summary of Events and Information	Remarks and references to Appendices
August 1st – 11th	Resting usual training	
August 12th Saturday	Relieved the 63rd Bde T.M.B. Relief complete about 6 pm No firing was done during the night.	
August 13th Sunday	Was devoted to improvement of emplacements and dugouts which in every case were in a state of acute disrepair. In the afternoon some registering was done.	
August 14th Monday	The improvements with regard to the emplacements were continued and the rusty shells were cleaned. In the early morning No1 group fired a few rounds with good effect in retaliation to the enemy fire which immediately ceased. During the daytime our mortars were active replying to hostile fire. No firing during the night.	

(73989) W4141—463. 400,000. 9/14. H.&J.Ltd Forms/C. 2118/10.

Army Form C. 2118.

Instructions regarding War Diaries and Intelligence Summaries are contained in F. S. Regs., Part II. and the Staff Manual respectively. Title pages will be prepared in manuscript.

WAR DIARY
or
INTELLIGENCE SUMMARY.
(*Erase heading not required.*)

Hour, Date, Place	Summary of Events and Information	Remarks and references to Appendices
August 15th Tuesday	All guns registered on enemy front line system. Owing to wet weather one of the emplacements fell in and much work was needed to put it in a state of repair. During the evening fire was directed on a hostile working party which was dispersed.	
August 16th Wednesday	During the early morning No1 Group was called upon to retaliate and 29 rounds were fired in all with good result. The work, in the connection with dugouts & emplacements, was carried on and good progress was made,	

(73989) W4141—463. 400,000. 9/14. H.&J.Ltd. Forms/C. 2118/10.

Instructions regarding War Diaries and Intelligence Summaries are contained in F. S. Regs., Part II. and the Staff Manual respectively. Title pages will be prepared in manuscript.

WAR DIARY
or
INTELLIGENCE SUMMARY.
(Erase heading not required.)

Army Form C. 2118.

Hour, Date, Place	Summary of Events and Information	Remarks and references to Appendices
August 17th Thursday	All groups carried up ammunition to complete extra establishment. The morning was used for checking registrations which were found correct. No firing during the evening.	
August 18th, Friday	In retaliation to some hostile shelling and mortar activity, a combined effort of medium and light trench mortars bombarded the enemy's line for 20 minutes intensive. Much damage was done and his first trench must have suffered severely, if not in men certainly in material as all sorts of duckboards etc. were seen	

(73989) W4141—463. 400,000. 9/14. H.&J.Ltd. Forms/C. 2118/10.

Instructions regarding War Diaries and Intelligence Summaries are contained in F. S. Regs., Part II. and the Staff Manual respectively. Title pages will be prepared in manuscript.

WAR DIARY
or
INTELLIGENCE SUMMARY.
(*Erase heading not required.*)

Army Form C. 2118.

Hour, Date, Place	Summary of Events and Information	Remarks and references to Appendices
August 18th Friday (continued)	to be broken and cast about the ramparts. At one point a pair of trousers flew into the air but it was impossible to observe whether anybody was inside them. In all some 250 shells were fired and there was no retaliation — a gratifying feature! In the afternoon all groups were kept busy with the carrying fusing & detonating of shells. There was no firing during the night.	

(73989) W4141—463. 400,000. 9/14. H.&J.Ltd. Forms/C. 2118/10.

Instructions regarding War Diaries and Intelligence Summaries are contained in F. S. Regs., Part II. and the Staff Manual respectively. Title Pages will be prepared in manuscript.

WAR DIARY
or
INTELLIGENCE SUMMARY
(Erase heading not required.)

Army Form C. 2118

Place	Date	Hour	Summary of Events and Information	Remarks and references to Appendices
August 19th	Saturday		There was no firing during the morning but in the afternoon we fired a few rounds into the enemy trench at long intervals of time.	
August 20th	Sunday		This day was quiet. During the evening we fired a few rounds.	
August 21st	Monday		In retaliation for enemy 'minenwerfer' our No 1 group left its emplacement and proceeded to the front line where it dug itself in and opened a hot and very accurate fire upon the enemy front line traversing to a length of 250 yards. Much damage was done and much trench material was thrown into the air. Altogether we fired 300 rounds.	
August 22,	Tuesday		During the evening we fired a few rounds into his front line on a hostile M.G. Emplacement (suspected).	
August 23,	Wednesday		Relieved 9 a.m by S. A. (28th) Bde T.M.B.	
August 23-31st			Reading Usual Training	

R. P. Penning Capt
OC 26th T.M.B.

1875 Wt. W593/826 1,000,000 4/15 J.B.C. & A. A.D.S.S./Forms/C. 2118.

9th Divisional Artillery

9th DIVL. TRENCH MORTAR BATTERIES,

A U G U S T, 1 9 1 6.

Officer i/c A.G's Office.,
BASE.

Herewith War Diary of 9th Divl Trench Mortar Brigade, for month of August.

J Broadwood Lieut
for DAAQMG
for Major General.,
Commanding 9th (Scottish) Division.

8/9/1916.

HEADQUARTERS,
9th (SCOTTISH)
DIVISION.
No. 16/41
Date 8/9/16

Officer i/c A.G's Office.,
BASE.

Herewith War Diary of 9th Divl Trench Mortar Brigade, for month of August.

J Birchwood Lieut
for DAAGMG
for Major General.,

8/9/1916. Commanding 9th (Scottish) Division.

9th DA.

Herewith War Diary of this unit for the month of August.

J. Laidman
Capt. RA,
Comdg 9th T.M. Bde

9/9/16

Instructions regarding War Diaries and Intelligence Summaries are contained in F. S. Regs., Part II. and the Staff Manual respectively. Title Pages will be prepared in manuscript.

WAR DIARY
or
~~INTELLIGENCE SUMMARY~~
(Erase heading not required.)

9. Vol 2

Army Form C. 2118.

August

9th Div Trench Mortar Brigade

Place	Date	Hour	Summary of Events and Information	Remarks and references to Appendices
Monneval	1st Aug to 14th "		In rest. Carrying out instructions on 2" mortars. Signalling. Map reading and usual drills.	
Camblain	15th "		Moved to fresh billets and inspected mortar emplacements in Carency, Berthonval Sections	
Vimy Ridge	16th "		Went into action in new line in conjunction with 37th Div. T. M. Batteries.	
	17th to 24th "		Constructing emplacements in the line with view of supporting Infantry in attack. 16 emplacements built with bomb stores. Mens dug-out. Telephone dug-outs. Lines laid to Hdqrs in Zouave Valley and from there to O.P. in Alhambra. Constructing dump dug-out in O.P. and also O.P. itself.	
	25th "		Co-operated with Div. Artillery in wire cutting on front S.8.b.9½-2 to S.9.a.1.9. Much wire cut. No retaliation.	
	26th "		Wire cutting on front, but owing to high wind shooting rather erratic.	
	27th "		Wire cutting continued. 120 rounds fired. Much damage done. Retaliation very light with Minenwerfers.	
	28th "		Wire cutting on front. 101 rounds expended. Demolished 2 bomb stores in enemy. No retaliation.	
	29th "		Wire cutting but weather bad and observation difficult. 72 rounds expended. Patrols report many gaps in wire.	

1875 Wt. W593/826 1,000,000 4/15 J.B.C. & A. A.D.S.S./Forms/C. 2118.

Instructions regarding War Diaries and Intelligence Summaries are contained in F. S. Regs., Part II. and the Staff Manual respectively. Title Pages will be prepared in manuscript.

WAR DIARY
or
~~INTELLIGENCE SUMMARY~~
(Erase heading not required.)

Army Form C. 2118

Place	Date	Hour	Summary of Events and Information	Remarks and references to Appendices
Vimy Ridge.	30th Aug		Wire cutting. 49 rounds. 1 of which fell short. No damage to our trenches.	
	31st "		Wire cutting on front. 130 rounds fired. There is little or no retaliation to our fire and we have a decided supremacy in Mortar fire. The Mortar however does not answer truly to its deflection and this is a great defect which should be remedied. Ammunition good and is got up by means of light railway which is a decided help.	

1875 Wt. W593/826 1,000,000 4/15 J.B.C. & A. A.D.S.S./Forms/C. 2118.

9

Army Form C. 2118

Instructions regarding War Diaries and Intelligence Summaries are contained in F. S. Regs., Part II. and the Staff Manual respectively. Title Pages will be prepared in manuscript.

WAR DIARY
or
INTELLIGENCE SUMMARY
(Erase heading not required.)

Place	Date	Hour	Summary of Events and Information	Remarks and references to Appendices
In the Field	August 1st		At 1st Army Trench Mortar School	
	7th		Practice carried out on Range.	
	8th		Left 1st Army Trench Mortar School. Capt Hallowes and 2/Lieut Hawkins and left Section V/37 attached to 123 Brigade R.F.A. 2nd Lieut Fletch and Right Section attached to 124 Bde RFA.	
	10th		Started on position for one Gun at S 8 d 30.25 map 36c S.W. 1/10.000. Hut started in Valley for Trench Party	
	13th		Started on position S. 21 a 00.35 same map as above.	
	16th		9th Divn Relieved 37th Div., Trench Mortars of 37th Divn remained in the line	
	17th		Right and Left Sections V/37 moved to VILLERS-AU-BOIS.	
	18th		Position S 8 d. 30 25 abandoned by order of 9th Division.	
			Till 31st August everyone engaged on digging two positions. ~~next~~ (a) S 21 a 00 35 and assisting 9th division with position at S 14 d. 65 30.	
			R. J. Hawkins 2Lt for Capt Comm V/37 H.T.M.	

1875 Wt. W593/826 1,000,000 4/15 J.B.C. & A. A.D.S.S./Forms/C. 2118.

Army Form C. 2118

Instructions regarding War Diaries and Intelligence Summaries are contained in F. S. Regs., Part II. and the Staff Manual respectively. Title Pages will be prepared in manuscript.

WAR DIARY
or
INTELLIGENCE SUMMARY
(Erase heading not required.)

Place	Date 1916 Aug	Hour	Summary of Events and Information	Remarks and references to Appendices
Villers au Bois	1-11th		Constructing gun positions & magazines	
	12th		Registered No 1 & 2 guns on wire & Hun front line opposite S15 c.3.6 – Observation from front line close to Mandora – International Sap.	
	13th		Selected new O.P.	
	14th		Construction work & laying buried cable –	
	15th –	19th	Construction of gun emplacements & magazines	
	20th		Carrying ammunition –	
	15th		Firing at 11 p.m. Premature wounding Lt [illegible], Br Clapp & Gr McSherry & Gillerand –	
	16th –	20th	Rebuilding wrecked emplacement –	
	21st		Two R.A. subalterns of [illegible] Div. arrived; demanding 6 of my gun emplacements & dugout. All action of guns taken over by	

Army Form C. 2118.

Instructions regarding War Diaries and Intelligence Summaries are contained in F. S. Regs., Part II. and the Staff Manual respectively. Title Pages will be prepared in manuscript.

WAR DIARY
or
INTELLIGENCE SUMMARY
(Erase heading not required.)

D/37 Hows.

Place	Date	Hour	Summary of Events and Information	Remarks and references to Appendices
Villers au Bois	Aug 1916 21		an officer of 9th Div.	
	22	-29	Building 2 new emplacements; cutting deep narrow trench between gun positions, Constructing new magazines, burying cable.	
	27	8pm	Premature at muzzle of gun killing B^r Collins & wounding 2 O.R.	
	28		Gr Gibson died.	
	30th - 31		Rebuilding new & wrecked emplacement.	
			J. M. [illegible] [illegible] D/37 Hows.	

1875 Wt. W593/826 1,000,000 4/15 J.B.C. & A. A.D.S.S./Forms/C. 2118.

9th Divisional Artillery.

9th DIVL. TRENCH MORTAR BATTERIES,

S E P T E M B E R, 1 9 1 6.

Instructions regarding War Diaries and Intelligence Summaries are contained in F. S. Regs., Part II. and the Staff Manual respectively. Title pages will be prepared in manuscript.

WAR DIARY
or
INTELLIGENCE SUMMARY.
(Erase heading not required.)

T.M. Bde

Army Form C. 2118.

Hour, Date, Place	Summary of Events and Information	Remarks and references to Appendices
1-9-16. Vimy Ridge.	In conjunction with 37th Div'n. T. M's, working on new emplacements for preliminary bombardment of hostile trenches, from Twins Crater to S. 15. C. 5. 4. Wire cutting along the Divisional front. Average expenditure 200 - 300 rounds per day.	Vol 3
2-9-16. -"-	Do.	
3-9-16. -"-	Do. Wire cutting on Sap. S. 9. a. 1½. 9. for raiding purposes. Wire well cut to satisfaction of raiding party. Fired 47 rounds during raid, forming small barrage.	
4-9-16. -"-	Wire cutting along Divisional front.	
5-9-16. -"-	Do. Little retaliation from hostile minenwerfer.	
6-9-16. -"-	Wire cutting and trench demolishing. M.G. emplacement at S. 15. C. 5. 5. demolished.	
7-9-16. -"-	Wire cutting. one round fell 200 yards short.	
8-9-16. -"-	do on front S. 15. C. 1. 7. to S. 15. a. 1½. 0. for raid on hostile trenches. 8 Blind rounds.	
9-9-16. -"-	- Do - M. G. emps. S. 15. C. 4½. 4½. and S. 15. C. 2. 6. demolished. 2 rounds fired during the night with Temple Silencers.	
12-9-16. -"-	Wire cutting between Kennedy & Irish Craters for raid on hostile trenches. 2 Bomb stores destroyed, trenches damaged.	

(73989) W4141—463. 400,000. 9/14. H.&J.Ltd. Forms/C. 2118/10.

Instructions regarding War Diaries and Intelligence Summaries are contained in F. S. Regs., Part II. and the Staff Manual respectively. Title pages will be prepared in manuscript.

WAR DIARY
or
INTELLIGENCE SUMMARY.
(*Erase heading not required.*)

Army Form C. 2118.

Hour, Date, Place	Summary of Events and Information	Remarks and references to Appendices
13-9-16. Vimy Ridge.	Do. Wire thoroughly cut and Infantry satisfied. Raid complete success. 3 rounds fell 100 yards short. Hostile retaliation rather heavy.	
14-9-16. — " —	Wire cutting along Divisional front.	
15-9-16. — " —	Do. Shooting very effective.	
	Heavy T. M. Bty in action. Observation by Aeroplane + F.O.O. Target No. 9. 2 direct hits obtained. All rounds fell into hostile trenches.	Map. No. 44.
	Night firing with Medium + Temple Silencers. Silenced several Machine guns.	
16-9-16. — " —	Wire cutting along JACK + EARL.	
17-9-16. — " —	Wire cutting along Divisional front.	
18-9-16. — " —	Reconnoitring new positions South of "Tottenham Road" as Divisional front has been lengthened + new scheme for attack made out.	
	Wire cutting on remainder of front. Most of hostile wire badly damaged.	

(73989) W4141—463. 400,000. 9/14. H.&J.Ltd. Forms/C. 2118/10.

Army Form C. 2118.

WAR DIARY
or
INTELLIGENCE SUMMARY.
(*Erase heading not required.*)

Instructions regarding War Diaries and Intelligence Summaries are contained in F. S. Regs., Part II. and the Staff Manual respectively. Title pages will be prepared in manuscript.

Hour, Date, Place	Summary of Events and Information	Remarks and references to Appendices
19-9-16. Vimy Ridge.	Wire cutting along JACK and from Point 31 to 27. 2. O.R. of Y/9 accidentally wounded owing to premature burst. Emplacement damaged but detachment were under cover	Map. No. 44.
20-9-16. -"-	Registering hostile trenches.	
21-9-16. -"-	Working on new emplacements. Wire cutting from 37 to 41. Unsatisfactory shooting owing to bad charges.	
22-9-16. -"-	Do. Do.	
23-9-16. -"-	Night firing with Silencers. Very successful. Registering HANOVER by Aeroplane. satisfactory but slow. M.G. emp. hit but no damage done to it.	
24-9-16. -"-	Wire cutting on JACK + MARQUIS.	Map. No. 44.
25-9-16. -"-	Fired 110 rounds on HANOVER during raid on hostile trenches	-"-
26-9-16. -"-	Firing with Temple Silencer on S.15.C.5.4. - very accurate.	
27-9-16 -"-	Wire cutting on GARTER. Firing on hostile Minenwerfer. silenced same. Night firing on hostile T.M. emps. at S.9.C.3.5. Rather heavy retaliation but had "last word"	

(73989) W4141—463. 400,000. 9/14. H.&J.Ltd. Forms/C. 2118/10.

Instructions regarding War Diaries and Intelligence Summaries are contained in F. S. Regs., Part II. and the Staff Manual respectively. Title pages will be prepared in manuscript.

WAR DIARY
or
INTELLIGENCE SUMMARY.
(*Erase heading not required.*)

Army Form C. 2118.

Hour, Date, Place	Summary of Events and Information	Remarks and references to Appendices
28-9-16. Vimy Ridge.	Firing on hostile Minenwerfer & also hostile T.M. emplacements. Hostile T.M. activity in Carency II sector considerably curtailed.	
29-9-16. -"-	Working on emplacements.	
30-9-16. -"-	Do. Firing by silencer on S.15.d.0.8. extremely accurate.	

(73989) W4141—463. 400,000. 9/14. H.&J.Ltd. Forms/C. 2118/10.

9th Divisional Artillery

9th DIVISIONAL TRENCH MORTAR BATTERIES,

OCTOBER, 1916.

9th T.M.B.

Instructions regarding War Diaries and Intelligence Summaries are contained in F. S. Regs., Part I. and the Staff Manual respectively. Title Pages will be prepared in manuscript.

WAR DIARY
or
INTELLIGENCE SUMMARY
(Erase heading not required.)

9TH TRENCH MORTAR BRIGADE.
No. ....
Date. 2/11/16.

Army Form. C. 2118

Vol 4

Place	Date	Hour	Summary of Events and Information	Remarks and references to Appendices
Vimy.	1st Oct.		Wire cutting by 2" Mortars. 9.45 firing on "Ladder Crater" 12 rounds. 2 shots, one of which demolished a 2" emplacement. no casualties resulting therefrom. Firing with Temple silencer owing to flat ground. Shoot successful.	
–"–	2nd "		Wire cutting and Trench demolishing by Medium Batteries. 98 rounds expended.	
–"–	3rd "		– Do – left of Gunner Crater. 35 rounds fired. This was for proposed raid by 24th Division. 9.45 fired 3 rounds on Zero line, but had to discontinue owing to observation being curtailed, due to mist.	
–"–	4th "		Positions and Guns taken over by the 24th Division.	
–"–	5th "		Moved by Motor Lorries to Bajus.	
	6th "		In rest billets at Bajus.	
	7th "		–"– –"– –"– –"–	
	8th "		Moved by Motor Lorries to BERLINCOURT.	
	9th "		–"– –"– –"– –"– –"– MARAIS LE SEC. near DOULLENS.	
	10th "		Entrained at 6.45 P.M. at Doullens for FRECHINCOURT. Horse transport sent on by road.	
LE SARS LINE	11th "		O.C. reported to 9th D.A. for purpose of taking (LE SARS LINE) over from 47th Division.	
–"–	12th "		O.C. shewn over gun positions by 47th Division. 1 - 2" Medium Trench Mortar in the line firing "Gas" bombs.	
–"–	13th "		Personel arrived at Frechincourt. Established Hdqrs. in Mametz Wood.	

Army Form. C. 2118.

Instructions regarding War Diaries and Intelligence Summaries are contained in F. S. Regs., Part II. and the Staff Manual respectively. Title Pages will be prepared in manuscript.

WAR DIARY
or
INTELLIGENCE SUMMARY
(Erase heading not required.)

Place	Date	Hour	Summary of Events and Information	Remarks and references to Appendices
LE SARS LINE,	14th Oct.		Reconnoitred positions in the new line for 4 guns. X and Y Batteries took over the line.	
-"-	15th --		4 guns in position in support line. Sergt. Theobald. Z/9 killed.	
-"-	16th --		500 rounds of 2" Ammunition dumped at High Wood. Sent 200 to Railway Terminus near Eaucourt Abbaye. Infantry carrying party deliver 45 rounds at guns. This method is very faulty owing to large bodies of men congregating in one spot. 2nd/Lieut. E. H. Montgomery. R. F. A. x/9 and 2nd/Lieut. J. R. Tarras. R. F. A. x/9. killed by shell whilst walking along C.T.	
-"-	17th --		Delivered 135 rounds to Guns. 4 guns in action on hostile front line. 80 rounds fired. Little retaliation - mostly by our own guns. 5 men wounded. 1 Officer and 1 N.C.O. of carrying party killed owing to being caught in hostile "barrage".	
-"-	18th --		Attack on Snag Trench. Fired a salvo in accordance with orders, just prior to attack. Infantry held up by M. G. at Snag Trench. Impossible to switch 2" Mortars on to same	
-"-	19th --		Attack still held up by M. G. in Tail Trench. Heavies bombarding same.	
-"-	20th --		Tail Trench captured.	
-"-	21st --		Reconnoitring for new positions in Snag Trench. Communication Trenches in bad condition owing to our bombardment, prior to the attack. Had to cross the open to get into front line. This involved much difficulty in getting Guns into position.	

Army Form. C. 2118

Instructions regarding War Diaries and Intelligence Summaries are contained in F. S. Regs., Part II. and the Staff Manual respectively. Title Pages will be prepared in manuscript.

WAR DIARY
or
INTELLIGENCE SUMMARY
(Erase heading not required.)

Place	Date	Hour	Summary of Events and Information	Remarks and references to Appendices
LE SARS LINE.	22nd Oct.		2 2" Mortars in position in Snag Trench.	
– " –	23rd – " –		Fired 25 rounds on hostile "Loop Trench". Observation difficult and supply of ammunition hard to keep up.	
– " –	24th – " –		Rain all day which delayed further firing.	
– " –	25th – " –		Relieved by 50th T. M. Brigade.	
– " –	26th – " –		At rest billets in Mametz Wood.	
	27th – " –		Salvaging ammunition in and about High Wood.	
	28th – " –		– " – – " – – " – – " – – " –	
	29th – " –		– " – – " – – " – – " – – " –	
	30th – " –		Carrying out usual drills and fatigues at Hdqrs. Mametz Wood.	
	31st – " –		– " – – " – – " – – " – – " – – " – – " –	

2/11/1916.

J. A. Laidman
Capt. R. F. A.
Comd'g 9th Div'n. Trench Mortar Brigade.

5879 – Imp. des A. C. – 24-7-15

9th Divisional Artillery

9th DIVL. TRENCH MORTAR BATTERIES,

N O V E M B E R, 1 9 1 6.

9th T.M. Bde.

Instructions regarding War Diaries and Intelligence Summaries are contained in F. S. Regs., Part II. and the Staff Manual respectively. Title pages will be prepared in manuscript.

WAR DIARY

~~INTELLIGENCE SUMMARY~~.

(Erase heading not required.)

Army Form C. 2118.

Vol 5

Place	Date	Hour	Summary of Events and Information	Remarks and references to Appendices
	Nov 1916			
MAMETZ WOOD	1st to 12th inc.		"At rest."	
	13th		Moved to ST. GRATIEN by lorries. Party from each Bty marched to ST. GRATIEN. about 20 miles.	
ST. GRATIEN.	14th		"At rest" Lt. Price Jones. O.C. vice O.C. att. A/50.	
	15th		–"–	
	16th		–"–	
	17th		–"– No. 46588. Gnr Walker. J. M. charged with "attempted murder" and assaulting a "Superior Officer."	
	18th		–"– O.C. returned to T.M.B.	
	19th to 25th inc.		–"–	
	26th		Moved to MIRVAUX by lorries. Party from each Bty marched, about 4 miles.	
MIRVAUX.	27th		No. 46588. Gnr Walker. J. M. tried by F.G.C.M. at T.M.B. H.Q. Moved to VILLERS BOCAGE by lorries.	
	28th		Moved to BARLEY. (18) miles by lorries. Party from each Bty marched to BEAUVAL (about 8 miles) and were conveyed to BARLEY by lorries.	
	29th		Moved to HONVAL by lorries. Party from each Bty marched (about 8 miles) Moved on same day to CANETTEMONT. about 2 miles.	
CANETTEMONT.	30th		"At rest" in billets.	

A. Whalteman Brown 2nd/Lieut. R.F.A.
for Capt. R.F.A.
Comd'g 9th Div. T.M. Bde.

2353 Wt. W254-/1454 700,000 5/15 D. D. & L. A.D.S.S./Forms/C. 2118.

9th Divisional Artillery

9th DIVL. TRENCH MORTAR BATTERIES,

D E C E M B E R, 1 9 1 6.

9th T.M. Bde

Army Form C. 2118.

Vol 6.

Instructions regarding War Diaries and Intelligence Summaries are contained in F. S. Regs., Part II. and the Staff Manual respectively. Title pages will be prepared in manuscript.

WAR DIARY

~~or~~

~~INTELLIGENCE SUMMARY.~~

(Erase heading not required.)

Place	Date	~~Hour~~	Summary of Events and Information	Remarks and references to Appendices
	Dec 1916			
CANETTEMONT.	1st to 25th		In rest billets. (X/9 + Y/9 went on a 2" T.M. redrilling course at 3rd Army T.M. School from 10th to 18th)	
	26th		Moved by lorries to billets in ARRAS.	
ARRAS.	27th		Took over T.M's in line from 35th Divn. X/35 remained attached to 9th T.M.B. + fired 59 rounds cutting wire)	
	28th		X/35 fired 44 rounds on enemy wire, opening gap for raid. Z/9 fired 20 rounds registering. K Sector.	
	29th		Wire cutting by X/9.	
	30th		-- -- X/9 + Y/9. 50 rounds fired.	
	31st		V/9 fired 9 ~~rounds~~ at trenches on Cambrai Rd. + demolished a brick house + started a fire.	
	--		X/9 + X/35 fired 71 rounds, cutting enemy's wire.	

1/1/17.

H A Miele [signature]
Capt. R. G. A.
Comd'g 9th Divn T. M. Brigade

2353 Wt. W2544/1454 700,000 5/15 D. D. & L. A.D.S.S./Forms/C. 2118.

Brigade Major
Riding.

Herewith War Diary for the month of January for 9th T.M. Brigade

9TH
TRENCH MORTAR
BRIGADE.
No.
3/2/1917 Date.

H. A. Mc[illegible]
Capt. R. G. A.
Comd'g 9th T. M. Bde.

Instructions regarding War Diaries and Intelligence Summaries are contained in F. S. Regs., Part II and the Staff Manual respectively. Title pages will be prepared in manuscript.

WAR DIARY
or
~~INTELLIGENCE SUMMARY.~~
(Erase heading not required.)

9TH TRENCH MORTAR BRIGADE.

No. ....

Date. ....

Army Form C. 2118.

Vol 7

Place	Date	Hour	Summary of Events and Information	Remarks and references to Appendices
ARRAS.	1st Jan	1917.	X + Y Btys fired 111 rounds cutting wire. V/9 fired 20 rounds. Z/9 busy removing guns.	
	2nd		X Y + Z Btys --- 97 --- --- --- V/9 engaged repairing emplacements.	
	3rd		Medium Btys --- 135 --- --- --- V/9 fired 10 rounds at Machine Gun emplt.	
	4th		All Btys engaged in putting emplts in order shifting guns, beds etc.	
	5th		Medium Btys fired 76 rounds on enemy wire. V/9 fired 8 rounds destroying enemy trench.	
	6th		--- --- --- 244 --- cutting wire for raid. V/9 = 26 --- --- --- ---	
	7th		Y + Z Btys fired 165 rounds wire cutting. V/9 fired 16 rounds. X/9 engaged repairing emplacement.	
	8th		V + X Btys engaged putting emplacements in order. Y + Z fired 48 rounds on enemy wire.	
	9th		Medium Btys fired 88 rounds on gaps in wire. V/9 fired 12 rounds on T.M. emplacement.	
	10th		V Bty engaged repairing emplacement. X/9 working on permanent emplacement.	
			Y + Z fired 130 rounds wire cutting.	
	11th		Medium Btys fired 121 rounds wire cutting. V/9 fired 16 rounds on enemy trenches.	
	12th		V X + Y Btys engaged in repairing emplacements etc. Z/9 fired 15 rounds registering new position	
	13th		Medium Btys fired 165 rounds on enemy wire. X/9 had 2 Prematures wrecking the emplacements + killing 2 N.C.O's + wounding 1 Gunner. V/9 engaged repairing emplacement.	

Instructions regarding War Diaries and Intelligence Summaries are contained in F. S. Regs., Part II. and the Staff Manual respectively. Title pages will be prepared in manuscript.

WAR DIARY
or
~~INTELLIGENCE SUMMARY.~~
(Erase heading not required.)

9TH TRENCH MORTAR BRIGADE.
.... No.
Date.

Army Form C. 2118.

Place	Date	Hour	Summary of Events and Information	Remarks and references to Appendices
ARRAS.	14th		V + X Btys engaged repairing emplacements. Y + Z fired 37 rounds on enemy's wire. 18 Gunners (6 from V 4 each X Y + Z) sent to Field Btys R.F.A for a week's course in the Field Artillery. 18 Gunners from Field Btys arrived to undergo a week's course in Trench Mortars	
	15th		V/9 + X/9 handed over to 35th Divn. emplt's in 1 Sector. V handed over 2 Guns + X four guns. Y + Z fired 89 rounds wire cutting.	
	16th		V/9 fired 20 rounds on enemy's trench, Y + Z fired 73 rounds wire cutting.	
	17th		Y + Z fired 16 rounds registering	
	18th		V/9 fired 10 rounds. Y + Z fired 89 rounds wire cutting. Z/9 had a Premature wounding 1 N.C.O.	
	19th		2nd/Lieut. C. S. Hampshire R.F.A. O.C. Y/9 wounded.	
	20th		V/9 fired 20 rounds retaliation for minnenwerfer. Z/9 fired 60 rounds wire cutting. 2nd/Lt Greenall X/9 + 2nd/Lt. Young Z/9 proceeded to 3rd Army Trench Mortar School at Ligny st flochel to undergo a 10 days course. 2nd/Lt. Bave from D.A.C. temporarily attached to Z/9.	

2353 Wt. W2544/1454 700,000 5/15 D. D. & L. A.D.S.S./Forms/C. 2118.

Instructions regarding War Diaries and Intelligence Summaries are contained in F. S. Regs., Part II. and the Staff Manual respectively. Title pages will be prepared in manuscript.

WAR DIARY
or
INTELLIGENCE SUMMARY.
(Erase heading not required.)

9TH TRENCH MORTAR BRIGADE.

No. .... Date.

Army Form C. 2118.

Place	Date	Hour	Summary of Events and Information	Remarks and references to Appendices
ARRAS.	21st		Y + Z fired 145 rounds programme. 18 Gunners returned from Field Btys & 18 Gunners returned to same.	
	22nd		V fired 20 rounds on enemy trenches. Y/9 fired 41 rounds wire cutting. 1 Gnr killed servant to 2/Lt. Price Jones	
	23rd		Y + Z fired 28 rounds cutting wire.	
	24th		Y/9 fired 25 rounds. Z/9 engaged shifting guns etc to new positions.	
	25th		V/9 fired 23 rounds destroying enemy trench. Y + Z fired 48 rounds registering + wire cutting	
	26th		-- -- 8 -- counter offensive. Y + Z fired 88 rounds cutting gaps in wire.	
	27th		-- -- 30 -- operation order. Y/9 fired 41 rounds offensive.	
	28th		-- -- 10 -- against minnenwerfer. Y + Z fired 123 rounds wire cutting	
			Another 18 Gnrs sent to Field Btys (as before) + 18 received from same for 1 week's course.)	
	29th		V/9 fired 16 rounds programme shoot. Y + Z fired 109 rounds as per programme.	
	30th		-- -- 10 -- on enemy trench. Y + Z fired 30 rounds wire cutting.	
			2nd/Lt Greenall X/9 + 2nd/Lt Young returned from 3rd Army Trench Mortar School.	
			2nd/Lt Cave returned to B.A.C.	
	31st		V/9 fired 15 rounds operation order. Y + Z fired 81 rounds wire cutting + offensive.	

F A Mullin[?] Capt. RGA

No 9 T.M.B. 2-2-17

9th T M Bde

Instructions regarding War Diaries and Intelligence Summaries are contained in F. S. Regs., Part II. and the Staff Manual respectively. Title pages will be prepared in manuscript.

WAR DIARY
or
~~INTELLIGENCE SUMMARY.~~
(Erase heading not required.)

Army Form C. 2118.

Vol 8

Place	Date	Hour	Summary of Events and Information	Remarks and references to Appendices
ARRAS	FEB 1st		V/9 fired 14 rounds counter offensive to enemy's minenwerfer. Y+Z Btys fired 81 rounds wire cutting	
	2nd		--- --- 13 --- destroying enemy's trenches. Y+Z Btys fired 69 rounds on enemy trenches + wire.	
	3rd		V/9 engaged putting emplacements in order. --- --- --- 61 --- --- --- --- ---	
	4th		Y+Z Btys fired 71 rounds destroying enemy wire. 18 Gunners sent to Field Btys for 1 weeks course and 18 Gunners received from Field Btys for 1 week's course in Trench Mortars.	
	5th		V/9 fired 17 rounds on enemy trenches. Y+Z Btys fired 79 rounds as per programme.	
	6th		V/9 --- 19 --- --- --- --- + houses, destroying 1 house. Y+Z Btys fired 40 rounds making gaps in wire.	
	7th		V/9 --- 9 --- --- --- trench. Y+Z Btys fired 113 rounds on wire doing considerable damage.	
	8th		Y+Z Btys fired 114 rounds making gaps in enemy wire.	
	9th		Y Bty fired 67 rounds on enemy trenches with good effect.	
	10th		2nd/Lieut. T.E. KENNARD. R.F.A. V/9 proceeded on T.M. course at 3rd Army Trench Mortar School.	
			V/9 fired 20 rounds destroying trenches and blowing up ~~a~~ house. Y+Z Bty Y+Z Btys fired 73 rounds as per programme	
	11th		18 Gunners returned from Field Btys after 1 weeks course + 14 Gnrs sent for same. 18 Gunners from Field Btys returned after 1 week's course in T.M's + another 18 received for same.	
			V/9 + Y/9 engaged repairing emplacements + re-laying beds. X+Z Btys fired 106 rounds on enemy wire.	

2353 Wt. W2544/1454 700,000 5/15 D. D. & L. A.D.S.S./Forms/C. 2118.

Army Form C.2118.

Instructions regarding War Diaries and Intelligence Summaries are contained in F. S. Regs., Part II. and the Staff Manual respectively. Title pages will be prepared in manuscript.

WAR DIARY
or
~~INTELLIGENCE SUMMARY.~~
(*Erase heading not required.*)

Place	Date	Hour	Summary of Events and Information	Remarks and references to Appendices
ARRAS	FEB 12th		V/9 fired 9 rounds destroying trench. Y + Z fired 78 rounds cutting enemy wire.	
	13th		V/9 --- 13 --- knocking a house down. X Y + Z Btys fired 174 rounds destroying sap + trenches.	
	14th		No 48459 Gnr TAYLOR J. Z/9 and Gnr MOSS J.J. A/51st Bde att. to Z/9 wounded.	
			V/9 fired 14 rounds in support of raid. X Y + Z Btys fired 429 rounds barrage for raid	
	15th		V/9 --- 17 --- demolishing trench. Y Bty fired 20 rounds wire cutting.	
	16th		V/9 --- 29 --- on enemy trenches. Y Bty fired 45 rounds retaliation to enemy H.T.M.	
	17th		V/9 + X/9 engaged repairing emplacements. Y + Z Btys fired 96 rounds on enemy wire + trench.	
	18th		V/9 + X/9 --- --- --- Y + Z Btys fired 51 rounds wire cutting + destroying sap.	
			No 4397 Gnr J. THOMAS. Z/9 killed + No 61617 Gnr J. SHIMMIN Z/9 wounded.	
			14 men returned from Field Btys after 1 week's course + 18 men returned to same after 1 week's course in T.M's	
	19th		V/9 fired 20 rounds destroying minenwerfer emplacement. Y + Z Btys fired 138 rounds cutting enemy wire.	
			No 132317 Gnr HARRIS W. J. V/9 + No 78762 Dvr THOMPSON J. V/9 wounded.	
	20th		V/9 fired 30 rounds on enemy trenches. Y + Z Btys. Y + Z Btys fired 80 rounds wire cutting.	
	21st		V/9 --- 33 --- destroying trenches. Y + Z Btys fired 101 rounds making gaps in wire	
			No 29284. Sergt. WARD W. A. Y/9 wounded.	
	22nd		V/9 fired 30 rounds blowing up 2 houses. Z/9 fired 80 rounds cutting enemy wire.	

2353 Wt. W2544/1454 700,000 5/15 D. D. & L. A.D.S.S./Forms/C. 2118.

Army Form C. [illegible]118.

Instructions regarding War Diaries and Intelligence Summaries are contained in F. S. Regs., Part II. and the Staff Manual respectively. Title pages will be prepared in manuscript.

WAR DIARY
or
~~INTELLIGENCE SUMMARY.~~

(Erase heading not required.)

Place	Date	Hour	Summary of Events and Information	Remarks and references to Appendices
ARRAS	FEB 23rd		V/9 fired 34 rounds on enemy trenches. Y + Z Btys fired 39 rounds registering + firing on enemy supports. No. 132202 Gnr NORTH A. killed (V/9)	
	24th		V/9 fired 22 rounds with good effect. X + Y Btys fired 61 rounds cutting enemy wire.	
	25th		V/9 --- 20 --- knocking 1 house down. X + Y Btys fired 125 rounds on enemy's wire + trenches.	
	26th		V/9 --- 12 --- on enemy trench. X, Y, + Z Btys fired 103 rounds with good effect on enemy wire.	
	27th		V/9 --- 16 --- shooting effective. X and Y Btys fired 83 rounds barrage for raid + making gap in wire	
	28th		V/9 --- 30 --- doing considerable damage. Y + Z Btys fired 148 rounds making gaps for raid.	

9TH
TRENCH MORTAR
BRIGADE.
.... No.
.... Date.

K A [illegible]
Capt RGA
3-3-17 OC 9th T.M.B.

2353 Wt. W2544/1454 700,000 5/15 D. D. & L. A.D.S.S./Forms/C. 2118.

9th TMs

Instructions regarding War Diaries and Intelligence Summaries are contained in F. S. Regs., Part II. and the Staff Manual respectively. Title pages will be prepared in manuscript.

WAR DIARY
or
INTELLIGENCE SUMMARY.
(Erase heading not required.)

9 D.T.M Bty
Vol 9

Army Form C. 2118.

Place	Date	Hour	Summary of Events and Information	Remarks and references to Appendices
ARRAS.	Mar 1st		Y/9 fired 70 rounds enlarging Gap. V/9. X/9. + Z/9 engaged preparing emplacements etc.	
			2nd/Lieut. W. D. Fisher proceeded on course at 3rd Army T.M. School Ligny St Flochel.	
	" 2		V/9 fired 13 rounds on strong points with good effect. X/9 + Y/9 fired 17 rounds, registration Z/9 engaged repairing emplacements.	
	" 3		Y/9 fired 20 rounds cutting a gap. V/9. X/9 + Z/9 putting emplacements in order.	
			2nd/Lieut. G. V. Greenall. R.F.A. X/9 transferred to A/51st Bde. R.F.A.	
	" 4		Y/9 fired 3 rounds registration. V/9. X/9 + Z/9 not firing.	
	" 5		V/9 fired 21 rounds on support trenches with good effect. X/9 + Y/9 fired 110 rounds with good results	
	" 6		V/9 fired 7 rounds on Trench junction. X/9 + Y/9 fired 38 rounds wire cutting + registration	
			2nd/Lieut. A. E. Latham Brown R.F.A. Y/9 transferred to B/51st Bde. R.F.A.	
	" 7		V/9 fired 12 rounds on enemy trench. X, Y + Z/9 fired 66 rounds wire cutting.	
	" 8		V/9 engaged repairing emplacements. X, Y + Z/9 fired 150 rounds wire cutting + making gaps.	
	" 9		V/9 " " " X. Y + Z/9 fired 130 rounds with good results.	
			No 137317. Gunner H. Taylor V/9 killed.	
	" 10		V/9 fired 16 rounds with good effect. Medium Batteries fired 122 rounds with good results	
			2 Medium Btys, X + Y, + 1 heavy V/18 from 18th Division attached to 9th T.M.B.	
			2nd/Lieut. W. D. Fisher returned from 3rd Army T.M. School after undergoing course in T.M's	

2353 Wt. W2544,1454 700,000 5/15 D. D. & L. A.D.S.S./Forms/C. 2118.

Instructions regarding War Diaries and Intelligence Summaries are contained in F. S. Regs., Part II. and the Staff Manual respectively. Title pages will be prepared in manuscript.

WAR DIARY

~~or~~

~~INTELLIGENCE SUMMARY.~~

(Erase heading not required.)

Army Form C. 2118.

Place	Date	Hour	Summary of Events and Information	Remarks and references to Appendices
ARRAS.	Mar. 11th		V/9 engaged repairing emplacements. Medium Batteries fired 150 rounds damaging enemy wire.	
	-- 12th		V/9 fired 11 rounds destroying enemy trench X/9, Y/9, Z/9 + X/18 fired 143 rounds cutting gaps in wire.	
			2nd/Lieut. W. Frew R.F.A. from A/51st Bde posted to X/9. Lieut. C.A. Lewis R.F.A. from A/50th Bde posted to Y/9.	
	-- 13th		X, Y + Z/9 + X + Y/18 fired 214 rounds making gaps in wire. V/9 repairing emplacements.	
	-- 14th		Y/9, Z/9 + X/18 fired 86 rounds with good results. V/9, X/9 + Y/18 not firing. V/18 fired 10 rounds registration	
	-- 15th		X Y + Z/9, X + Y/18 fired 217 rounds cutting wire. V/18 fired 8 rounds on enemy trench. V/9 not firing.	
	-- 16th		Y + Z/9 + X + Y/18 fired 158 rounds making gaps in wire. V/9, X/9 + V/18 not firing.	
	-- 17th		X, Y + Z/9, X + Y/18 fired 226 rounds with good effect. V/9 fired 10 rounds on enemy trench. V/18 not firing	
	-- 18th		X, Y + Z/9, X + Y/18 fired 344 rounds making gaps in wire. V/18 fired 4 rounds registration. V/9 not firing	
	-- 19th		X, Y + Z/9, X + Y/18 fired 286 rounds with good effect. V/9 + V/18 not firing.	
	-- 20th		X, Y + Z/9, X + Y/18 fired 346 rounds making further gaps. V/9 + V/18 not firing	
	-- 21st		X, Y + Z/9, X + Y/18 fired 304 rounds wire cutting with good effect. V/9 fired 19 rounds on enemy trenches	
			V/18 not firing. No. 149248 Gnr. J. Simpson R.F.A. Y/9 wounded + died after admission to Hospital	
	-- 22nd		X + Y/9, X + Y/18 fired 270 rounds damaging wire. V/18 fired 10 rounds registration. V/9 not firing.	
	-- 23rd		X, Y + Z/9, X + Y/18 fired 469 rounds cutting gaps in wire. V/9 + V/18 fired 10 rounds each, registration.	
			4th Division T.M. Brigade attached to 9th T.M. Brigade. No. 89667 Cpl W. Lawrence V/9 wounded 22/3/17	

Army Form C. 118.

Instructions regarding War Diaries and Intelligence Summaries are contained in F. S. Regs., Part II. and the Staff Manual respectively. Title pages will be prepared in manuscript.

WAR DIARY

~~or~~

~~INTELLIGENCE SUMMARY.~~

(Erase heading not required.)

Place	Date	Hour	Summary of Events and Information	Remarks and references to Appendices
ARRAS.	Mar 24th		X. Y + Z/9. + X + Y/18 fired 348 rounds, cutting enemy wire. V/18 fired 5 rounds. V/9 did not fire. No 10193. Pte T. Healy Z/9 T.M.B. killed. 1 Officer (2nd Lieut. W. J. Francis 12th Royal Scots) and 52 men Infantry attached to V/9.	
	-- 25th		X. Y + Z/9. X + Y/18 + X + Z/4 fired 368 rounds making gaps in wire. V/9 fired 10 rounds doing considerable damage.	
	-- 26th		X. Y + Z/9. X + Y/18 + X + Z/4 fired 348 rounds cutting wire and enlarging gaps. V/18 + V/4 fired 5 rounds each registering + destroying trench. V/9 did not fire.	
	-- 27th		X Y + Z/9. X + Y/18 + Z/4 fired 225 rounds with satisfactory results. V/18 fired 10 rounds + V/4. 5 rounds with good effect. V/9 did not fire. Y/18 had a premature resulting in the death of No 26189. Corporal W. W. Waters + wounding No 1666 Gnr S. S. Horton + damaging the emplacement.	
	-- 28th		X Y + Z/9. X/18. + X + Z/4 fired 446 rounds with good results. V/9 fired 14 rounds + V/4 fired 8 rounds doing considerable damage. V/18 did not fire. Y/18 engaged repairing emplacement. No 15090 Pte A. Roff 8th Black Watch. No 2238 Pte R. Smith 5th Camerons + No 8046 Pte A. McGill 10th A + S.H. attached to V/9 wounded.	
	-- 29th		X. Y + Z/9. X/18. + X + Z/4 fired 442 rounds cutting wire. Heavy Btys V/9. V/18 + V/4 did not fire.	
	-- 30th		X. Y + Z/9. X/4 + Z/4 fired 356 rounds with good results. V/9 fired 23 rounds on enemy trench. Z/9 had emplacement partially blown in. No 29608 Act/Bdr J. McLeod. No 57482, Gnr G. Smith. contd	

Army Form C. 2118.

Instructions regarding War Diaries and Intelligence Summaries are contained in F. S. Regs., Part II. and the Staff Manual respectively. Title pages will be prepared in manuscript.

WAR DIARY

~~or~~

~~INTELLIGENCE SUMMARY.~~

(Erase heading not required.)

Place	Date	Hour	Summary of Events and Information	Remarks and references to Appendices
ARRAS	Mar 30th	cont^d	+ No 18512 Cpl D. Johnstone Z/9 and No 95990. Gnr J. McAndrews Y/9 wounded.	
			V/4, V/18 + X + Y/18 did not fire.	
	31st		Y + Z/9. X/18. X + Z/4 fired 350 rounds damaging enemy wire. V/18 fired 15 rounds on enemy trench with good effect. V/9 + V/4 did not fire.	

9TH
TRENCH MORTAR
BRIGADE.
No.
3/4/1917 Date.

H A Mull
Capt. R. G. A.
Comd'g 9th Divn T.M. Bde.

2353 Wt. W2544/1454 700,000 5/15 D. D. & L. A.D.S.S./Forms/C. 2118.

9th Bde

Instructions regarding War Diaries and Intelligence Summaries are contained in F. S. Regs., Part II. and the Staff Manual respectively. Title pages will be prepared in manuscript.

WAR DIARY
or
~~INTELLIGENCE SUMMARY.~~
(Erase heading not required.)

Army Form C. 2118.

Vol 10

Place	Date	Hour	Summary of Events and Information	Remarks and references to Appendices
ARRAS	1st April		Y/9 + Z/9, X/18, X/4 + Z/4 fired 296 rounds making gaps in enemy wire. V/9 + V/18 fired 52 rounds on enemy trenches with good effect. X/9, Y/18 + V/4 did not fire. 37th Divn T.M. Brigade arrived in ARRAS and attached to 9th T.M. Bde	
	2nd		X/9, Y/9, Z/9, X/18, X/4, Z/4 + Y/37 fired 368 rounds wire cutting with good result. V/18 fired 11 rounds on enemy trench. V/9, Y/18, + V/4 did not fire.	
	3rd		X/9, Z/9, X/4 + Z/4 fired 191 rounds making + enlarging gaps in wire. V/9, Y/9, V/18, X/18, Y/18, V/4 + Y/37 not firing.	
	4th		First day of Bombardment. V day. Medium Batteries comprising X, Y + Z/9, X + Y/18, X + Z/4, Y/37 + Z/37 fired 1959 rounds. V/9 + V/18 fired 205 rounds. V/4 + V/37 not firing.	
	5th		2nd day of Bombardment. W day. Medium Batteries fired 1966 rounds. Heavy Batteries fired 558 rounds. 1 N.C.O. + 2 Gnrs X/9 slightly wounded. No 184998 Gnr J.O. Evans Y/9 wounded	
	6th		3rd day of Bombardment. X day. Medium Batteries fired 1706 rounds. Heavy Batteries fired 410 rounds. No 130084. Gnr D. West. Y/9 wounded.	
	7th		4th day of Bombardment. Q day (extra day) Medium Batteries fired 1732 rounds. Heavy Batteries fired 377 rounds.	
	8th		5th day of Bombardment. Y day. Medium Batteries fired 1991 rounds. Heavy Batteries fired	

2353 Wt. W2544/1454 700,000 5/15 D. D. & L. A.D.S.S./Forms/C. 2118.

Continued

Instructions regarding War Diaries and Intelligence Summaries are contained in F. S. Regs., Part II. and the Staff Manual respectively. Title pages will be prepared in manuscript.

WAR DIARY
or
~~INTELLIGENCE SUMMARY.~~
(*Erase heading not required.*)

Army Form C. 2118.

Place	Date	Hour	Summary of Events and Information	Remarks and references to Appendices
ARRAS.	8th	Continued	605 rounds. Lieut Maclure X/18 wounded slightly. Cpl Pelse, Gnr Owens, Gnr Long & Gnr [illegible] all of X/4 killed. Gnrs Holgate & Mellor Z/37 & Gnr Downie Y/37 wounded.	
	9th		"Z" day. Medium Batteries fired 219 rounds & Heavy Batteries fired 132 rounds previous to the advance & also to assist Artillery barrage. Lieut H. W. Taylor O.C. X/9 wounded. Gnr Hannahes V/37 & Gnrs Downey, Dunne, Smith, Bishop & Castle V/18 wounded.	
	10th		All Batteries engaging in removing guns from emplacements & shifting same to clean, cleaning same etc. Personnel returned to billets in ARRAS. No 138802 Gnr W. A. Ward X/9 to Hospital with shell shock.	
	11th		9th T.M. Bde & detachment from 4th T.M. Bde took over captured German Guns & went into action fired 2 rounds 8", 40 rounds 5.9, & 60 rounds 77 m.m. Lieut T. H. Hawkins Z/4 Cpl Simpson V/9 Dr Burgess V/9 Gnr Mallinson Y/4 Gnr Dunbar Z/4 & Gnr Boyce V/4 wounded	
	12th		Fired 8 rounds 8", 80 rounds 5.9 and 480 rounds 77 m.m. (captured German Guns)	
	13th		-- 3 -- 8" 30 -- 5.9 -- 60 -- 77 m.m. -- -- --	
	14th		-- 89 rounds 5.9 & 30 rounds 77 m.m.	
	15th		-- 40 -- 5.9 & 60 rounds 77 m.m. Gnr Williams V/9 wounded	
	16th		-- 50 -- 5.9 & 200 -- 77 m.m.	

Instructions regarding War Diaries and Intelligence Summaries are contained in F. S. Regs., Part II. and the Staff Manual respectively. Title pages will be prepared in manuscript.

WAR DIARY
~~or~~
~~INTELLIGENCE SUMMARY.~~
(Erase heading not required.)

Army Form C. 2118.

Place	Date	Hour	Summary of Events and Information	Remarks and references to Appendices
ARRAS	17th April		Batterys resting in Billets	
	18th		— — — —	
	19th		— — — — Bdr. C. Wright X/9 Bty admitted to Hospital (wounded 15th inst)	
	20th		— — — —	
	21st		— — — — Pte M. Young 12th Royal Scots killed. Pte R. Laighton 12th Royal Scots Pte W. Fleming 5th Camerons Pte G. Powell 5th Camerons Pte W. Kilpatrick 6th K.O.S.B. wounded. All attached to V/9. Casualties caused by enemy shell bursting in billet whilst men were sleeping.	
	22nd		Batterys resting in Billets 1 N.C.O + 12 men sent to 9th D.A. Hdqrs for fatigues for the day	
	23rd		— — — — — — — — — — — —	
	24th		— — — — Lt. Francis + Infantry attached to V/9 returned to their Regiments	
	25th		— — — — 2 Sergts 2 Bdrs + 16 Gunners sent to 50th Bde R.F.A. 16 Gunners sent to 51st Bde R.F.A. 1 N.C.O + 12 men sent to 9th D.A. Hdqrs for fatigues for the day	
	26th		Batterys resting in Billets — — — — — — — —	
	27th		20 Gunners sent to 51st Bde R.F.A. 1 N.C.O. + 12 men sent to 9th D.A. Hdqrs for fatigues for day.	
	28th		1 N.C.O + 12 men sent to 9th D.A. Hdqrs for fatigues for day.	

Instructions regarding War Diaries and Intelligence Summaries are contained in F. S. Regs., Part II. and the Staff Manual respectively. Title pages will be prepared in manuscript.

WAR DIARY
or
INTELLIGENCE SUMMARY.
(Erase heading not required.)

Army Form C. 2118.

Place	Date	Hour	Summary of Events and Information	Remarks and references to Appendices
ARRAS.	29th April		13 Gunners sent to 50th Bde R.F.A. 1 N.C.O. + 12 men sent to 9th D.A. Hdqrs for fatigues for day.	
			2nd/Lieut. W. D. Fisher R.F.A. Z/9. transferred to D/52nd Bde R.F.A.	
			Gnr Shipman Y/9 attached to 50th Bde wounded. Gnrs Mawson + Neary V/9 att to B/51st Bde wounded	
	30th --		9 Gunners sent to 50th Bde R.F.A. 1 N.C.O + 12 men sent to 9th D.A. Hdqrs for fatigues for day	
			Gnr. Potter Y/9 att. to 50th Bde wounded (69th) Gnr Treson V/9 att. to B/51st Bde wounded	

9TH TRENCH MORTAR BRIGADE.
.................No.
4/5/17.......Date

K A Muckle
Capt R.F.A.
Cmd of 9th Div T M Bde

2353 Wt. W2544/1454 700,000 5/15 D. D. & L. A.D.S.S./Forms/C. 2118.

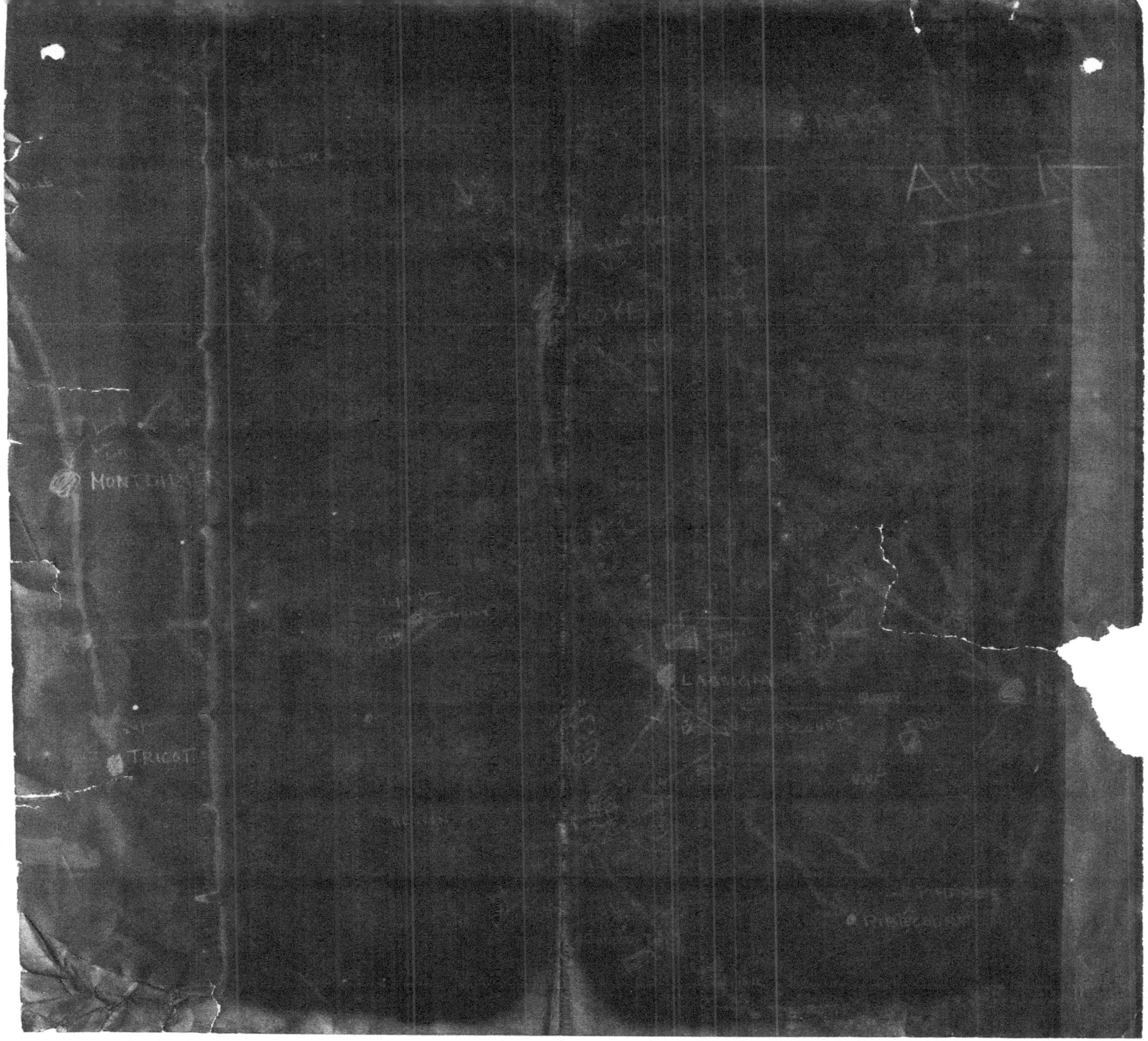

9th T M Bde

Instructions regarding War Diaries and Intelligence Summaries are contained in F. S. Regs., Part II. and the Staff Manual respectively. Title pages will be prepared in manuscript.

WAR DIARY
or
INTELLIGENCE SUMMARY.
(Erase heading not required.)

Army Form C. 2118.

9 D T M Bty
Vol XI

Place	Date	Hour	Summary of Events and Information	Remarks and references to Appendices
ARRAS	May 1st		6 N.C.O's + 14 men sent to 9th D.A. Hdqrs for the day (fatigues.) Gnr Watson X/9 att to D/51st Bde wounded, died in Hospital. Gnrs Smith, Wilson + Mc Ewan Z/9 all attached to D/51st Bde killed.	
	" 2nd		5 N.C.O's + 14 men sent to 9th D.A. Hdqrs for the day (fatigues.) Lt. Young Z/9 attached to B/50th Bde. 2nd/Lt Kennard V/9 attached to C/50th Bde.	
	" 3rd		9 N.C.O's + 11 Gunners sent to 9th D.A. Hdqrs for the day (fatigues.) Gnr Smith Y/9 attached to D/51st Bde wounded.	
	" 4th		6 N.C.O's + 16 Gunners sent to 9th D.A. Hdqrs for the day (fatigues.)	
	" 5th		9 " + 14 " " " " " " "	
	" 6th		5 " + 17 " " " " " " " " Gnr Ware V/9 att to D/50 wounded	
	" 7th		At rest in billets Personnel engaged salving 2" bombs + component parts	
	" 8th		" " " Lt. W. Price Jones Y/9 transferred to Kite Balloon Section. R.F.C. Personnel	
	" 9th		" " " " Gnr Paynter Y/9 att to D/50th Bde killed. engaged in salving 2" bombs.	
	" 10th		" " " " Personnel engaged salving 2" ammunition.	
	" 11th		" " " " Bdr Falla V/9 att to A/50th Bde wounded. Personnel engaged salving bombs	
	" 12th		" " " " Personnel engaged salving 2" bombs + spare parts.	

2353 Wt. W2544/1454 700,000 5/15 D. D. & L. A.D.S.S./Forms/C. 2118.

Instructions regarding War Diaries and Intelligence Summaries are contained in F. S. Regs., Part II. and the Staff Manual respectively. Title pages will be prepared in manuscript.

WAR DIARY
~~or~~
~~INTELLIGENCE SUMMARY.~~
(Erase heading not required.)

Army Form C. 2118.

Place	Date	Hour	Summary of Events and Information	Remarks and references to Appendices
ARRAS	May 13th		At rest in billets. Personnel engaged salving 2" bombs + spare parts	
	-- 14th		-- -- -- -- -- -- -- -- -- -- --	
	-- 15th		-- -- -- -- -- -- -- -- -- -- --	
	-- 16th		-- -- -- -- -- -- -- -- -- -- --	
	-- 17th		-- -- -- -- 2nd/Lieut. W. Reid transferred to B/51st Bde.	
	-- 18th		-- -- -- -- Personnel engaged salving 2" bombs + spare parts	
	-- 19th		-- -- -- -- -- -- -- -- -- --	
	-- 20th		-- -- -- -- Gnr Nicholls X/9 att. to D/51. Gnr Forbes V/9 att. to C/51 Gnr Leverett V/9 att. to D/50. Gnr Johnson V/9 att. to B/51 + Gnr Birket V/9 att. to C/50 all wounded.	
	-- 21st		At rest in billets. Personnel engaged salving 2" bombs	
	-- 22nd		-- -- -- -- -- -- -- -- --	
	-- 23rd		-- -- -- -- Lt. W. Price Jones from Kite Balloon Section. R.F.C. 20 men sent to D.A.C. fatigues.	
	-- 24th		Brigade moved to ANZIN ST. AUBIN. Lt. W. Price Jones to Hospital (sick)	
ANZIN.ST.AUBIN	-- 25th		At rest in billets. Personnel engaged in cleaning up stores, etc	
	-- 26th		-- -- -- -- Personnel attached to Field Btys returned to 9th T.M.B. Casualties to 9th T.M. Bde personnel whilst att. to Field Btys. 4 men killed, 2 men wounded, died in Hospital, 12 men wounded + 1 man sent to Hospital sick.	

2353 Wt. W2544/1454 700,000 5/15 D. D. & L. A.D.S.S./Forms/C. 2118.

Army Form C. 2118.

Instructions regarding War Diaries and Intelligence Summaries are contained in F. S. Regs., Part II. and the Staff Manual respectively. Title pages will be prepared in manuscript.

WAR DIARY
or
INTELLIGENCE SUMMARY.
(Erase heading not required.)

Place	Date	Hour	Summary of Events and Information	Remarks and references to Appendices
[A]NZIN ST [A]UBIN.	May 27th		At rest in billets. Lt. G. A. Young returned from S/55th Bde. 8 Officers from 9th D.A.C. att. to 9th T.M.B. for instruction in 2" + 9.45	
	28th		— — — Personnel engaged cleaning guns etc.	
	29th		— — — Personnel engaged on Gun Drill, Telephone instruction etc.	
	30th		— — — — — — — — —	
	31st		— — — — — — — — —	

H A Mickle
Capt. R. G. A.
Comd'g 9th Divn. T. M. Brigade.

9TH TRENCH MORTAR BRIGADE.
.... No.
4/6/17 .... Date.

2353 Wt. W2544/1454 700,000 5/15 D. D. & L. A.D.S.S./Forms/C. 2118.

9th T M Bde

Instructions regarding War Diaries and Intelligence Summaries are contained in F. S. Regs., Part II. and the Staff Manual respectively. Title pages will be prepared in manuscript.

WAR DIARY
~~or~~
~~INTELLIGENCE SUMMARY.~~

(Erase heading not required.)

Army Form C. [illegible]118.

Vol 12

Place	Date	Hour	Summary of Events and Information	Remarks and references to Appendices
[...]NZIN ST AUBIN.	1st June		At rest. — During this period Personnel engaged in 2" & 9.45 Gun Drill Gas Helmet Drill Rifle & Marching Drill, Swedish Drill etc.	
	2nd		---	
	3rd		--- Lt. W. Price Jones from Hospital.	
	4th		---	
	5th		---	
	6th		---	
	7th		---	
	8th		---	
	9th		---	
	10th		---	
	11th		---	
	12th		---	
	13th		--- Lt. G. A. Young to Hospital Sick.	
	14th		Brigade moved to FOUFFLIN RICAMETZ.	
[...]OUFFLIN - [...]ICAMETZ	15th		At rest. Lt. C. A. Lewis & Cpl Owen to 3rd Army Gas School. 2nd/Lieut T. Lewis, 2nd/Lieut. T. R. Scott, & 2nd/Lieut J. Kennedy to 3rd Army Trench Mortar School.	

2353 Wt. W2544/1454 700,000 5/15 D. D. & L. A.D.S.S./Forms/C. 2118.

Instructions regarding War Diaries and Intelligence Summaries are contained in F. S. Regs., Part II. and the Staff Manual respectively. Title pages will be prepared in manuscript.

WAR DIARY
or
INTELLIGENCE SUMMARY.
(Erase heading not required.)

Army Form C. 2118.

Place	Date	Hour	Summary of Events and Information	Remarks and references to Appendices
FOUFFLIN RICAMETZ.	16th June		At rest	During this period Personnel engaged in 2" + 9.45 Gun Drill, Gas Helmet Drill, Rifle + Marching Drill, Swedish Drill, etc.
	17th --		-- --	
	18 --		-- --	
	19th --		-- --	
	20th --		-- --	
	21st --		-- -- Lt. Lewis + Cpl Owen returned from 3rd Army Gas School.	
	22nd --		-- -- Lt. G. A. Young from Hospital.	
	23rd --		-- --	
	24th --		-- --	
	25th --		-- --	
	26th --		D.T.M.O. + Officers Y/9 Bty + 6 OR from V/9 moved to ARRAS.	
ARRAS.	27th --		Remainder of Brigade moved to ARRAS. Y/9 relieved Y/61 in the line, taking over two 2" Guns + V/9 relieved V/61 taking over one 9.45 in the line.	
ACHICOURT.	28th		Brigade moved to ACHICOURT, taking over billets from 61st T.M. Bde. 1 Cpl + 20 men sent to Brigade Major 167th Infantry Brigade to collect dud ammunition. Y/9 fired 8 rounds registering	
	29th		Y/9 fired 20 rounds on shell holes. 1 Cpl + 20 men sent for the day to collect dud ammunition.	

Instructions regarding War Diaries and Intelligence Summaries are contained in F. S. Regs., Part II and the Staff Manual respectively. Title pages will be prepared in manuscript.

WAR DIARY
or
INTELLIGENCE SUMMARY.
(Erase heading not required.)

Army Form C. 2118.

Place	Date	Hour	Summary of Events and Information	Remarks and references to Appendices
ACHICOURT	30th June		Y/9 fired 5 rounds. 1 Cpl + 20 men sent for the day to collect dud ammunition 2nd/Lieut. F. A. Richards, 2nd/Lieut. J. G. Hickman + 2nd/Lieut. W. A. Sweet-Escott to 3rd Army Trench Mortar School.	

9TH TRENCH MORTAR BRIGADE.
No. ....
Date. 1/7/1917

H A Mickle
Capt. R. G. A.
Comdg 9th T. M. Brigade

2353 Wt. W2544/1454 700,000 5/15 D. D. & L. A.D.S.S./Forms/C. 2118.

9th T M Bde

Instructions regarding War Diaries and Intelligence Summaries are contained in F. S. Regs., Part II. and the Staff Manual respectively. Title pages will be prepared in manuscript.

WAR DIARY
or
~~INTELLIGENCE SUMMARY.~~

(Erase heading not required.)

Army Form C. 2118.

9 D T M Btys

8 of 13

Place	Date	Hour	Summary of Events and Information	Remarks and references to Appendices
ACHICOURT	1st July		Y/9 fired 30 rounds on enemy in Shell Holes with good effect V/9 fired 10 rounds on enemy trench with good results. No. 47395. Corpl G.E. DICKENSON. R.G.A. Y/9 killed by a premature. 1 Cpl + 10 men sent for the day to Bde Major 168th Bde, burying duds. 1 Bdr + 10 men sent for the day to Town Major ACHICOURT burying duds.	
	2nd		9th Divn T.M. Brigade relieved in the line by 12th Divn T.M. Brigade handing over one 9.45 + 2 2" Guns. 1 Cpl + 10 men sent for the day to Adjutant 56th Div'l Train + 1 Bdr + 10 men sent for the day to Town Major ACHICOURT burying duds.	
	3rd		1 Cpl + 20 men sent for the day to Bde Major 168th Bde, burying duds.	
	4th		At Rest	
	5th		Brigade moved to WANQUETIN	
WANQUETIN	6th		At Rest.	
	7th		-- --	
	8th		-- -- During this period Personnel engaged in Gun Drill,	
	9th		-- -- Box Respirator Drill, Rifle + Marching Drill, instructed	
	10th		-- -- in Map reading etc.	
	11th		-- --	
	12th		-- --	

Instructions regarding War Diaries and Intelligence Summaries are contained in F. S. Regs., Part II. and the Staff Manual respectively. Title pages will be prepared in manuscript.

WAR DIARY

~~or~~

~~INTELLIGENCE SUMMARY.~~

(Erase heading not required.)

Army Form C. 2118.

Place	Date	Hour	Summary of Events and Information	Remarks and references to Appendices
WANQUETIN	13th July		Annual Sports of the 9th T.M. Bde	
	14th		2nd/Lieut F.A. Richards, 2nd/Lieut J.G. Hickman & 2nd/Lieut W.A. Sweet Escott returned from course at 3rd Army Trench Mortar School	
	15th		At Rest	
	16th		-- --	
	17th		-- --	
	18th		V/9 moved to BOIRY BECQUERELLE and attached to 50th Division'l Artillery	
			X/9 & Z/9 Btys moved to HAMELINCOURT and attached to 21st Divisional Artillery	
			The above mentioned Bty's engaged from 18th to 31st inst on fatigues for 50th D.A & 21st D.A respectively, constructing gun positions etc	
			2/Lieut J.G. Hickman, 2nd/Lieut W.A. Sweet Escott, 2nd/Lieut F.A. Richards 2nd/Lieut J. DeCaubingue, & 2nd/Lieut C.G.F. Wickham attached to 50th Brigade R.F.A	
	19th to 31st inc.		Y/9 T.M. Bty at rest. Bty engaged in 2" Gun Drill, Box Respirator Drill, etc	

9TH TRENCH MORTAR BRIGADE.
No. ....
Date 1/8/1917

[signature]
Capt. R.G.A.
Comd of 9th Div. T.M. Bde

2353 Wt. W2544/-454 700,000 5/15 D. D. & L. A.D.S.S./Forms/C. 2118.

Instructions regarding War Diaries and Intelligence Summaries are contained in F. S. Regs., Part II. and the Staff Manual respectively. Title pages will be prepared in manuscript.

9" T.M's

WAR DIARY
or
INTELLIGENCE SUMMARY.
(Erase heading not required.)

Army Form C. 2118.

Vol 9/14

Place	Date	Hour	Summary of Events and Information	Remarks and references to Appendices
WANQUETIN	Aug 1st		Y/9 at rest. X + Z/9 Btys attached to 21st D.A. + V/9 attached to 50th D.A. for fatigues.	
	2nd		—	
	3rd		Y/9 moved to VALLUART WOOD Map reference P.33.a. (Sheet 57C) + were joined by X + Z/9 Btys from 21st D.A. + V/9 from 50th D.A. Brigade took over camp vacated by 58th T.M.Bde + took over 1 9.45 gun	
VALLUART WOOD	4th		Brigade engaged in putting Camp in order + cleaning up same.	
	5th		Relieved 3rd Div T.M. Bde in the line taking over 1 9.45 gun + exchanging 3 2" Mortars for 3 in the line, belonging to 3rd T.M.Bde.	
	6th		Detachments from V/9 + Y/9 take over dug outs in the line.	
	7th		Brigade engaged on fatigues in the camp.	
HAVRINCOURT WOOD	8th		Headquarters moved to HAVRINCOURT WOOD. Map reference Q.1.a.0.9. Y/9 fired 8 rounds at Midnight, retaliation to hostile minnenwefer	
	9th		Nothing to report.	
	10th		X + Z Btys + detachments from Y + V Btys numbering 50 men sent to 50th + 51st Bdes R.F.A. 2nd Lieut L.E. Jenkinson R.F.A. transferred to Royal Flying Corps.	
	11th		Y/9 fired 5 rounds at midnight, offensive.	
	12th		Y/9 fired 10 rounds 12-30 AM. at Sniper's Post	

2333 Wt W2544/1454 700,000 5/15 D. D. & L. A.D.S.S./Forms/C. 2118.

Army Form C. 2118.

Instructions regarding War Diaries and Intelligence Summaries are contained in F. S. Regs., Part II. and the Staff Manual respectively. Title pages will be prepared in manuscript.

WAR DIARY
~~or~~
~~INTELLIGENCE SUMMARY.~~

(Erase heading not required.)

Place	Date	Hour	Summary of Events and Information	Remarks and references to Appendices
HAVRINCOURT WOOD.	Aug 13th		Y/9 unable to fire owing to Infantry Patrols being out.	
	14th		Y/9 fired 5 rounds at 11.15 PM. 53 O.R. R.F.A. from 3rd Army Trench Mortar School attached to 9th T.M. Bde.	
	15th		Personnel returned from 50th & 51st Bdes. sent on 11th inst.	
	16th		Relieved 42nd T.M. Bde in TRESCAULT & HAVRINCOURT SECTORS & were relieved by 42nd T.M. Bde in HERMIES SECTOR. V/9 fired 9 rounds at 1.45 am co-operating in a raid. Y/9 fired 3 rounds. Took over 2 9.45s from 42nd T.M. Bde.	
	17th		Z/9 fired 24 rounds on WIGAN COPSE & ETNA CRATER registration & offensive.	
	18th		Z/9 fired 62 rounds on DEAN & WIGAN COPSE, assisting bombardment previous to raid. V/9 fired 21 rounds at 10.58 PM to 11.25 PM assisting the raid.	
	19th		Z/9 fired 30 rounds on ETNA & WIGAN COPSE with good results at 5 & 9 P.M.	
	20th		V/9 fired 8 rounds with good results. Z/9 fired 94 rounds destroying enemy trenches. 2nd Lieut. G. Buttle R.F.A. transferred to Royal Flying Corps. Relieved 42nd T.M. Bde in HERMIES SECTOR.	
	21st		Y/9 fired 12 rounds & Z/9 2 rounds retaliation to minnenwerfer. X/9 relieved Y/9 in the line.	
	22nd		X/9 fired 10 rounds offensive which drew heavy enemy retaliation. Z/9 fired 27 rounds (25 with Thermite bombs) in Wigan & Dean Copse to ignite brushwood, but though successful in reaching targets bombs failed to ignite.	

2353 Wt. W2544/1454 700,000 5/15 D. D. & L. A.D.S.S./Forms/C. 2118.

Army Form C. 2118.

Instructions regarding War Diaries and Intelligence Summaries are contained in F. S. Regs., Part II. and the Staff Manual respectively. Title pages will be prepared in manuscript.

WAR DIARY
~~or~~
~~INTELLIGENCE SUMMARY.~~

(*Erase heading not required.*)

Place	Date	Hour	Summary of Events and Information	Remarks and references to Appendices
HAVRINCOURT WOOD.	Aug 23rd		V/9 fired 20 rounds on suspected Minnenwerfer emplt ~~at [illegible]~~ X/9 fired 3 rounds + Z/9 20 rounds on enemy wire.	
	" 24th		V/9 fired 30 rounds on Minnenwerfer emplt. Z/9 fired 15 rounds on WIGAN + DEAN COPSE + X/9 15 rounds at intervals from 9 PM to 4 AM.	
	" 25th		V/9 fired 12 rounds, Z/9 fired 35 rounds + X/9 21 rounds. X/9 silencing hostile minnenwerfer	
	" 26th		Z/9 fired 23 rounds on Quarry with good effect. X/9 fired 12 rounds during the night. V/9 did not fire.	
	" 27th		Z/9 fired 28 rounds on enemy wire, with good results, gaps being made. V/9 + X/9 did not fire. No 15687 Cpl. S. J. Jones R.F.A. + No 110407 Gnr Godward R.F.A. Z/9 wounded by Premature.	
	" 28th		Z/9 fired 67 rounds on enemy wire + Wigan Copse with good effect. V/9 + X/9 did not fire	
	" 29th		Z/9 fired 77 rounds on enemy wire with good results. V/9 + X/9 did not fire	
	" 30th		Z/9 fired 70 rounds wire cutting + in support of raid. V/9 fired 6 rounds at 3.30 p.m for registering 9.45" MK III Trench Mortar + 20 rounds T.M.F. in support of raid	
	" 31st		V/9 fired 6 rounds on R.27.b.6.2. with 9.45" T.M. MK III	

[signature] Capt R.F.A.
Comdg 9th Div Trench Mortar Brigade

2353 Wt. W2544/1454 700,000 5/15 D. D. & L. A.D.S.S./Forms/C. 2118.

9th T.M. Bde

Instructions regarding War Diaries and Intelligence Summaries are contained in F. S. Regs., Part II. and the Staff Manual respectively. Title pages will be prepared in manuscript.

WAR DIARY ~~or~~ INTELLIGENCE SUMMARY.

(Erase heading not required.)

Army Form C. 2118.

9 D T M Bty

Vol 15

Place	Date	Hour	Summary of Events and Information	Remarks and references to Appendices
HAVRINCOURT WOOD	1st Sept		Relieved by the 36th Divn T.M. Bde in the line. Handed over five 9.45 T.Ms	
			Brigade moved to RUYAULCOURT	
RUYAULCOURT	2nd --		At RUYAULCOURT	
	3rd --		Brigade moved to SAPIGNIES, encamped at H 7 b 4 6.	
SAPIGNIES	4th --		In Camp.	
	5th --		-- --	
	6th --		-- -- Draft of 30 men joined Brigade from 9th D.A.C.	
	7th --		Entrained at BAPAUME in two parties. Advanced party of 1 Officer & 3 O.R. having left in morning	
	8th --		Detrained at POPERINGHE & moved by lorries to K3 central approx. (Sheet 57 c)	
NEAR WATOU	9th --		In Camp.	
	10th --		-- --	
	11th --		-- --	
	12th --		Brigade moved to new camp situated at K.2. c. 3.5.	
	13th --		In Camp.	
	14th --		-- --	
	15th --		-- --	

2353 Wt. W2544/1454 700,000 5/15 D. D. & L. A.D.S.S./Forms/C. 2118.

Instructions regarding War Diaries and Intelligence Summaries are contained in F. S. Regs., Part II. and the Staff Manual respectively. Title pages will be prepared in manuscript.

WAR DIARY

~~or~~

~~INTELLIGENCE~~ SUMMARY.

(Erase heading not required.)

Army Form C. 2118.

Place	Date	Hour	Summary of Events and Information	Remarks and references to Appendices
NEAR WATOU	16th Sep		In Camp. Lieut Young R.F.A. + 50 O.R. attached to 50th Bde R.F.A. Lieut T.A. Lewis R.F.A. + 50 O.R. attached to 51st Bde. R.F.A.	
	17th		In Camp	
	18th		-- --	
	19th		-- --	
	20th		-- --	
	21st		-- --	
	22nd		-- --	
	23rd		-- --	
	24th		-- -- Capt Mickle R.G.A. returned from Officers Convalescent Home & resumed command of Brigade.	
	25th		-- --	
	26th		-- -- Lieut W. Price Jones R.F.A. Lieut R. Wylie R.F.A. + 2nd/Lieut C.A.R. Kennedy R.F.A. att. to 9th D.A.C.	
	27th		-- --	
	28th		-- --	
	29th		Brigade moved to 9th D.A.C. camp situated at G10. d. (Sheet 28)	
NEAR POPERINGHE	30th		In Camp	

9TH TRENCH MORTAR BRIGADE. 30/9/1917. Date.

K.A. Mickle
Capt R.G.A.
Cmd'g 9th Divn T.M. Brigade

Instructions regarding War Diaries and Intelligence Summaries are contained in F. S. Regs., Part II. and the Staff Manual respectively. Title pages will be prepared in manuscript.

9th T.M.

WAR DIARY
or
~~INTELLIGENCE SUMMARY~~

(Erase heading not required.)

Army Form C. 2118.

9 D T M Btys

Vol 16

Place	Date	Hour	Summary of Events and Information	Remarks and references to Appendices
NEAR POPERINGHE	1st Oct		Brigade in Camp with 9th D.A.C. (At rest 100 O.R. being attached to Field Btys)	
	2nd --		In Camp. Capt K. A. Mickle DTMO to 5th Army T.M. School	
	3rd --		-- --	
	4th --		-- --	
	5th --		-- --	
	6th --		Brigade moved to HAM HOEK A 25. b 2½ 3 Sheet 28	
HAM HOEK	7th --		In Camp	
	8th --		-- -- Capt K. A. Mickle DTMO returned from 5th Army T M School	
	9th --		-- --	
	10th --		-- --	
	11th --		-- --	
	12th --		-- --	
	13th --		-- --	
	14th --		-- --	
	15th --		-- --	
	16th --		-- --	

2353 Wt. W2544/1454 700,000 5/15 D. D. & L. A.D.S.S./Forms/C. 2118.

Army Form C. 2118.

Instructions regarding War Diaries and Intelligence Summaries are contained in F. S. Regs., Part II. and the Staff Manual respectively. Title pages will be prepared in manuscript.

WAR DIARY
or
INTELLIGENCE SUMMARY.
(Erase heading not required.)

Place	Date	Hour	Summary of Events and Information	Remarks and references to Appendices
HAM HOEK	17th Oct		In Camp.	
	18th --		-- -- 2nd/Lieut. T. E. Kennard R.F.A. to Royal Flying Corps. 2nd/Lieut T. R. Scott R.F.A. att. to C/50th Bde. R.F.A.	
	19th --		-- --	
	20th --		-- --	
	21st --		-- --	
	22nd --		Brigade moved to GHYVELDE area.	
GHYVELDE AREA	23rd --		In Camp.	
	24th --		-- --	
	25th --		-- --	
	26th --		-- --	
	27th --		-- --	
	28th		-- -- Personnel returned from Field Btys. The following casualties were incurred by this unit whilst attached to same. Lieut. G. A. Young R.F.A. Z/9 T.M.B. Missing believed killed. Killed in action Cpl Scott, Gnrs Pearman, Jones, & Armstrong V/9. Gnr Cole Y/9. Gnr Gorlett Z/9. Died after admission to Hspital Gnrs Lines & Warburton V/9. Wounded. Bdr Garner, Gnrs Goldbey, Broadbridge, Preston, Ingold, Mason, Seymour, Jones W. Jones E. J. Rogers, Raynor, Smith & Ryder V/9	
			Contd.	

2353 Wt. W2544/1454 700,000 5/15 D. D. & L. A.D.S.S./Forms/C. 2118.

Instructions regarding War Diaries and Intelligence Summaries are contained in F. S. Regs., Part II. and the Staff Manual respectively. Title pages will be prepared in manuscript.

WAR DIARY
or
INTELLIGENCE SUMMARY.
(Erase heading not required.)

Army Form C. 2118.

Place	Date	Hour	Summary of Events and Information	Remarks and references to Appendices
GHYVELDE AREA	28th Oct	Contd	Gnrs Brown, Bennett + Buckley + Land X/9. Gnrs Moore Monger + Pte Boulter Y/9. Bde Morris Gnrs Chafey, Sairne, Oatley Mooney + Kite Z/9. To Hospital sick Gnr Knowles X/9 + McMillan Z/9. Died in Billet, Gnr Murphy X/9. Total 1 Officer, 37 O.R.	
	29th		Brigade moved to COXYDE BAINS + relieved 41st Div T.M. Bde in the line.	
COXYDE BAINS	30th		Personnel engaged in preparing gun-pits, checking ammunition etc.	
	31st		V/9 fired 4 rounds retaliation on hostile T.M. emplt. Y/9 fired 12 rounds NEWTON 6" ~~offensive~~ retaliation	

9TH TRENCH MORTAR BRIGADE.
.... No.
1/11/17 .... Date.

H.A. Michle
Capt R.G.A.
Comd'g 9th Div T.M. Brigade.

2353 Wt. W2534/1454 700,000 5/15 D. D. & L. A.D.S.S./Forms/C. 2118.

Instructions regarding War Diaries and Intelligence Summaries are contained in F. S. Regs., Part II. and the Staff Manual respectively. Title pages will be prepared in manuscript.

WAR DIARY
or
INTELLIGENCE SUMMARY.
(Erase heading not required.)

Army Form C. 2118.

9 DTM Bn
Vol 17

Place	Date	Hour	Summary of Events and Information	Remarks and references to Appendices
COXYDE BAINS.	1st Nov	1917	V/9 fired 2 rounds retaliation. Y/9 fired 57 rounds NEWTON 6" offensive & retaliation good effect	
	2nd --		V/9 -- 2 -- -- Y/9 -- 50 -- -- -- retaliation. X/9 fired 13 rounds 2" registration.	
	3rd --		V/9 fired 6 rounds retaliation. Y/9 fired 40 rounds NEWTON 6" retaliation.	
	4th --		V/9 -- 5 -- Y/9 fired 40 rounds NEWTON 6", & X/9 fired 12 rounds 2" retaliation. No. 129436 Gnr. H. KNOWLES R.F.A. V/9 killed in action.	
	5th --		V/9 fired 24 rounds retaliation good effect. Y/9 fired 66 rounds retaliation on enemy emplacements with good results. X/9 fired 3 rounds 2" registration.	
	6th --		V/9 fired 2 rounds retaliation. Y/9 fired 8 rounds NEWTON 6" & X/9 8 rounds 2" retaliation.	
	7th --		V/9 fired 1 round testing gun on new position. X/9 personnel engaged in rebuilding gun pit blown in by enemy. Y/9 did not fire standing by in case of need.	
	8th --		V/9 & Y/9 did not fire standing by. X/9 fired 2 rounds testing extreme switch.	
	9th --		V/9 fired 3 rounds retaliation. X/9 fired 3 rounds 2" retaliation. Y/9 did not fire.	
	10th --		No Battery did any firing this day owing to Infantry reliefs taking place.	
	11th --		Y/9 fired 4 rounds registration on hostile T.M. emplt. V/9 & X/9 did not fire.	
	12th --		V/9 fired 2 rounds retaliation & Y/9 5 rounds retaliation on hostile T.M.	

2353 Wt. W2544/1454 700,000 5/15 D. D. & L. A.D.S.S./Forms/C. 2118.

Instructions regarding War Diaries and Intelligence Summaries are contained in F. S. Regs., Part II. and the Staff Manual respectively. Title pages will be prepared in manuscript.

WAR DIARY
or
INTELLIGENCE SUMMARY.
(Erase heading not required.)

Army Form C. 2118.

Place	Date	Hour	Summary of Events and Information	Remarks and references to Appendices
COXYDE BAINS	13th Nov		Y/9 fired 25 rounds NEWTON 6" on hostile T.M. empl't's good effect V/9 + X/9 did not fire	
	14th "		Y/9 " 35 " " " 6 " " " " " " V/9 + X/9 " " "	
	15th "		No firing took place X/9 engaged on removing ammunition to salvage + guns from the line +	
	16th "		No firing took place X/9 + Y/9 engaged in removing ammunition to salvage	
	17th "		Y/9 fired 10 rounds on hostile T.M. V/9 engaged in removing ammunition + guns	
	18th "		V/9 fired 2 rounds Y/9 fired 1 round. Relieved in the line by the 29th French Artillery during the night of 18th + 19th inst handing over 1 French H.T.M. + 43 heavy bombs	
	19th "		Personnel engaged in removing guns from the line + sending same to XI Corps Ordnance ammunition returned to salvage. 2 2" Mortars sent to 2nd Army T.M. School	
	20th "		At rest in billets	
	21st "		" " " "	
	22nd "		Brigade moved in lorries to BEAURAINVILLE (2nd Army Area)	
BEAURAINVILLE	23rd to 30th ult		At rest During this period Brigade engaged in Gun Drill, Box Respirator Drill, Rifle + March Drill etc.	

9TH TRENCH MORTAR BRIGADE.
No.
3/12/17 Date.

H. A. Muckle
Capt R. G. A.
Comd'g 9th Div'n T.M. Brigade

2353 Wt. W2541/1454 700,000 5/15 D. D. & L. A.D.S.S./Forms/C. 2118.

9. T.M.

Instructions regarding War Diaries and Intelligence Summaries are contained in F. S. Regs., Part II. and the Staff Manual respectively. Title Pages will be prepared in manuscript.

WAR DIARY
or
INTELLIGENCE SUMMARY
(Erase heading not required.)

9TH TRENCH MORTAR BRIGADE. ......No. 1/1/18 ......Date.

Army Form. C. 2118

VR/18

Place	Date	Hour	Summary of Events and Information	Remarks and references to Appendices
BEAURAINVILLE	1st Dec	1917	Brigade moved by Motor Lorries to WAMIN, entrained at the latter place during the night in 3 trains at different hours for DOINGT.	
DOINGT	2nd --		Brigade arrived + fixed up in camp.	
	3rd --		In camp.	
	4th --		-- --	
	5th --		-- --	
	6th --		-- --	
	7th --		Brigade moved by Motor Lorries to HEUDICOURT.	
HEUDICOURT	8th --		Brigade engaged on salvage work at GOUZEAUCOURT.	
	9th --		-- -- -- -- -- -- --	
	10th --		-- -- -- -- -- -- Steam-Roller salved on this date.	
	11th --		-- --	
	12th --		--	
	13th --		-- -- --	
	14th --		--	
	15th --		--	
	16th --		-- -- Capt. J. MAC MURRAY R.F.A. O.C. V/9 admitted to Hospital, wounded, whilst engaged in salvage operations.	
	17th		Brigade engaged on salvage work at GOUZEAUCOURT	

Instructions regarding War Diaries and Intelligence Summaries are contained in F. S. Regs., Part II. and the Staff Manual respectively. Title Pages will be prepared in manuscript.

WAR DIARY

~~or~~

INTELLIGENCE SUMMARY

(Erase heading not required.)

Army Form. C. 2118

Place	Date	Hour	Summary of Events and Information	Remarks and references to Appendices
HEUDICOURT	18th Dec	1917	Brigade engaged in salvage work at GOUZEAUCOURT. Caravan salved on this date.	
	19th ..			
	20 ..			
	21st ..		2nd Lt [illegible] SWEET-ESCOTT R.F.A. posted to 50th Bde R.F.A.	
			1 N.C.O + 9 men sent to 9th D.A. for fatigues.	
	22nd ..		Detachment from Y/9 went into the line taking over 2 6" NEWTONS at the Quarry. Salvage work also engaged upon.	
	23rd ..		1 N.C.O. + 9 men sent to 9th D.A. for fatigues	
	24th ..		Steam Roller No 2 finally salved on this date.	
	25th ..		CHRISTMAS DAY	
	26th ..		1 N.C.O. + 9 men sent to 65th Bde. R.F.A. for fatigues. Salvage work also engaged upon	
	27th ..		Also work completed of sand-bagging all Huts + shelters in the camp commenced 21st.	
	28th ..		1 N.C.O + 9 men sent to 65th Bde. R.F.A for fatigues. Salvage work also engaged upon. Also work commenced on dug-outs in camp.	
	29th ..		Y/9 fired 13 rounds registration. Fatigue party sent to 65th Bde R.F.A. as usual + work continued on dug-outs.	
	30th ..		Fatigue party sent to 65th Bde. R.F.A + work continued on dug-outs	
	31st ..			

K A Mickle Capt R.G.A.
Comd'g 9th Divn T.M. Brigade

9" T.M. Btie — Vol 19

Instructions regarding War Diaries and Intelligence Summaries are contained in F. S. Regs., Part II. and the Staff Manual respectively. Title pages will be prepared in manuscript.

WAR DIARY or ~~INTELLIGENCE SUMMARY.~~

(Erase heading not required.)

Army Form C. 2118.

Place	Date	Hour	Summary of Events and Information	Remarks and references to Appendices
HEUDICOURT	1st Jan. 1918		V/9 personnel at work on new gun emplt's. Medium Btys at work on dug-outs 1 N.C.O. & 9 men sent to 65th Bde R.F.A. fatigues for the day 2 9.45 guns taken over from 21st Divn.	
	2nd "		V/9 engaged on new gun emplts. also X/9. remainder of personnel at work on dug-outs	
	3rd "		" " " " " " " " " " " "	
	4th "		Y/9 fired 23 rounds 6" NEWTON registration. V/9 + X/9 at work on new gun emplts. Z/9 at work on dug-outs.	
	5th "		" " 8 " " " " " " " " " " " " " "	
			2/Lieut J. Tarr. R.F.A. + 8 O.R. sent to 5th Army T.M. School for course	
	6th "		Y/9 fired 17 rounds 6" NEWTON registering new gun in Quarry. V/9 + X/9 engaged as on 5th inst. also Z/9	
	7th "		V/9 + X/9 at work on new gun emplt's. Z/9 on dug-outs. Sgt Connelly, Bdr Locke, Gnr Alison, + Pte Richards, all of Y/9 + Gnr Fishlock V/9 wounded.	
	8th "		V/9 + X/9 at work on new gun emplt's, Z/9 engaged on new dug-outs.	
	9th "		" " " " " " " " " " "	
	10th		" " " " " " " " " " " "	
			Y/9 fired 14 rounds 6" NEWTON on enemy trenches with good results.	
	11th "		Y/9 " 13 " " " on enemy front line. V/9 + X/9 engaged as on 10th also Z/9 similarly employed.	
	12th "		Y/9 fired 20 rounds 6" NEWTON retaliation to enemy's 5.9's shelling GOUZECOURT. V/9, X/9 + Z/9 engaged as on 11th inst.	9

Army Form C. 2118.

WAR DIARY
or
~~INTELLIGENCE SUMMARY~~.
(Erase heading not required.)

Instructions regarding War Diaries and Intelligence Summaries are contained in F. S. Regs., Part I. and the Staff Manual respectively. Title pages will be prepared in manuscript.

Place	Date	Hour	Summary of Events and Information	Remarks and references to Appendices
[?]EUDICOURT	13th Jan	1918	Y/9 fired 20 rounds 6" NEWTON on enemy trench with good effect. X/9 + V/9 at work on new gun emplt's. Z/9 engaged on dug-outs	
	14th --		Y/9 fired 8 rounds 6" NEWTON checking registration. X/9 fired 4 rounds 6" NEWTON, registering gun. V/9 + Z/9 employed as on the 13th.	
	15th --		X/9 + V/9 working on gun pits. Z/9 upon dug-outs	
	16th --		X/9 fired 6 rounds 6" NEWTON registration. Z/9 + V/9 employed as on 15th.	
	17th --		All Btys engaged working upon new emplacements.	
	18th --		-- -- -- -- -- -- --	
	19th --		-- -- -- -- -- -- -- 2nd/Lieut. G. Tass R.F.A. + personnel returned from 5th Army T M School. Y/9 fired 6 rounds 6" NEWTON checking registration.	
	20th --		All Btys engaged working upon new emplacements.	
	21st --		-- -- -- -- -- -- Y/9 fired 6 rounds 6" NEWTON registration	
	22nd --		-- -- -- -- -- --	
	23rd --		-- -- -- -- -- --	
	24th --		-- -- -- -- -- -- Y/9 fired 9 rounds 6" NEWTON registration + checking same.	
	25th --		-- -- -- -- -- -- Y/9 -- 7 rounds -- --	

Instructions regarding War Diaries and Intelligence Summaries are contained in F. S. Regs., Part II. and the Staff Manual respectively. Title pages will be prepared in manuscript.

WAR DIARY

or

INTELLIGENCE SUMMARY.

(*Erase heading not required.*)

Army Form C. 2118.

Place	Date	Hour	Summary of Events and Information	Remarks and references to Appendices
HEUDICOURT	26th Jan	1918	Brigade engaged working upon new gun emplacements.	
	27th		Y/9 fired 20 rounds NEWTON 6" offensive with good effect. X/9. V/9 + Z/9 at work upon gun emplacements. Draft of 25 O.R. posted to this unit from 9th D.A.C.	
	28th		Y/9 fired 60 rounds NEWTON 6" at Infantry's request on suspected M.G. empt. good results were obtained. X/9. Z/9 + V/9 working on gun emplacements.	
	29th		V/9 fired 6 rounds 9.45 (Long) registration. Y/9 fired 81 rounds offensive on enemy's trenches, doing considerable damage to same. X/9 + Z/9 working on gun emplacements. Gnr. Oliver Y/9 killed in action.	
	30th		X/9 fired 10 rounds NEWTON 6" registering on enemy trench. Y/9 fired 46 rounds NEWTON 6" offensive, good effect. V/9 + Z/9 at work on gun emplacements.	
	31st		Y/9 fired 10 rounds NEWTON 6" offensive. V/9 X/9 + Z/9 working on gun emplacements. Lieut. W. Price Jones R.F.A. Y/9 + Pte Gooch Y/9 wounded.	

9TH TRENCH MORTAR BRIGADE.

.................No.

1/2/18 Date.

H A Meikle Capt R.F.A.
Comd'g 9th Div. T.M. Bde

93

Instructions regarding War Diaries and Intelligence Summaries are contained in F. S. Regs., Part II. and the Staff Manual respectively. Title pages will be prepared in manuscript.

WAR DIARY

~~or~~

~~INTELLIGENCE~~ SUMMARY.

(Erase heading not required.)

Army Form C. 2118.

9 D TM Bty

Vol 20

94

Place	Date	Hour	Summary of Events and Information	Remarks and references to Appendices
MARLEY CAMP	14th Feb	1918	In Camp. All R.G.A. personnel in 9th T.M. Bde transferred to VII Corps H.A.	
	15th --		-- }	
	16th --		-- } Personnel engaged on gun drill & instructed in the 6" NEWTON T.M.	
	17th --		-- }	
	18th --		-- }	
	19th --		-- Lieut C.A. Lewis, Lieut R. Wylie 2nd/Lieut G. Tass + 30 O.R. proceeded to V Army T.M. School to undergo course in 6" NEWTON T.M.	
	20th --		In Camp	
	21st --		--	
	22nd --		--	
	23rd --		-- Draft of 19 N.C.O's (10 Cpls + 9 Bdrs) from Base Details posted to this unit.	
	24th --		In Camp	
	25th --		--	
	26th --		-- 1 N.C.O. + 8 Gnrs transferred from 9th D.A.C. bringing the unit up to strength.	
	27th --		--	
	28th --		--	

H. A. Mitchell
Capt. R.G.A.
Comd'g 9th Div T.M. Bde

9TH
TRENCH MORTAR
BRIGADE.
28/2/18 Date.

2353 Wt. W2 [illegible] 11454 700,000 5/15 D. D. & L. A.D.S.S./Forms/C. 2118.

WAR DIARY
or
~~INTELLIGENCE SUMMARY.~~

(Erase heading not required.)

Army Form C. 2118.

Instructions regarding War Diaries and Intelligence Summaries are contained in F. S. Regs., Part II. and the Staff Manual respectively. Title pages will be prepared in manuscript.

Place	Date	~~Hour~~	Summary of Events and Information	Remarks and references to Appendices
HEUDICOURT	1st Feb	1918	All Btys engaged in building gun positions.	
	2nd --		-- -- -- -- -- -- --	
	3rd --		Medium Btys relieved in the line by 39th T. M. Bde. V/9 remaining in the line, & were transferred to VII Corps. H. A.	
	4th --		Brigade moved to MARLEY CAMP near BRAY SUR SOMME	
MARLEY CAMP	5th --		In Camp	
	6th --		-- -- During this period personnel were given instructions & undergone gun drill. in the 6" NEWTON. T M.	
	7th --		-- --	
	8th --		-- --	
	9th --		-- --	
	10th --		-- --	
	11th --		-- --	
	12th --		-- -- Lieut R. Wylie, 2nd/Lieut G. Tarr & 17 O.R. from V/9 rejoined 9th T.M. Bde. Lieut R. H. W. Davidson R.F.A. from B/51st Bde & 2nd/Lieut. H. W. Taylor R.F.A from Base Details posted to 9th T. M. Bde.	
	13th --		Brigade re-organised Z/9 Bty being disbanded the Bde consisting of 2 Btys X/9 & Y/9 under the new regime	

2353 Wt. W2544/1454 700,000 5/15 D. D. & L. A.D.S.S./Forms/C. 2118.

96

9th Div.

9th DIV. TRENCH MORTAR BRIGADE.

M A R C H

1 9 1 8

9th TM Bde

Instructions regarding War Diaries and Intelligence Summaries are contained in F. S. Regs., Part II. and the Staff Manual respectively. Title pages will be prepared in manuscript.

WAR DIARY
or
INTELLIGENCE SUMMARY.
(*Erase heading not required.*)

9 D T M Bty
Vol 21

Army Form C. 2118.

Place	Date	Hour	Summary of Events and Information	Remarks and references to Appendices
MARLEY CAMP NEAR BRAY.	1st Mar		Brigade moved to camp near HAUT ALLAINES. I 10 b. 6 3 sheet 62 c.	
HAUT ALLAINES	2nd ..		At rest. Capt Mickle DTMO to Hospital sick	
	3rd ..		.. .. Capt Taylor assumed duties of DTMO vice Capt Mickle.	
	4th ..		Brigade moved to camp near PERONNE I 27 a central sheet 62 c.	
NEAR PERONNE	5th ..		At rest	
	6th ..		..	
	7th ..		.. During this period personnel were given instruction	
	8th ..		.. + underwent drill with the 6" NEWTON TM	
	9th ..		..	
	10th ..		..	
	11th ..		Brigade moved to HEUDICOURT + relieved 39th Div. T.M. Bde taking over 10 6" NEWTONS + 5 Hotchkiss Anti Tank Guns in the line	
HEUDICOURT	12th ..			
	13th ..			
	14th ..			
	15th ..			

Army Form C. 2118.

Instructions regarding War Diaries and Intelligence Summaries are contained in F. S. Regs., Part II. and the Staff Manual respectively. Title pages will be prepared in manuscript.

WAR DIARY

~~or~~

~~INTELLIGENCE SUMMARY.~~

(Erase heading not required.)

Place	Date	Hour	Summary of Events and Information	Remarks and references to Appendices
HEUDICOURT	16th Mar		During the period from 12th to 21st Mar the 10 6" NEWTONS were registered on different points in enemy line. Personnel was also engaged detonating 2" bombs in mine field	
	17th			
	18th			
	19th			
	20th			
	21st		Enemy bombardment commenced. Gun positions all evacuated after rendering guns useless.	
	22nd		Brigade moved to FINS & from latter place to MOISLAINES	
	23rd		Brigade moved to COMBLES & from there to MONTAUBAN	
	24th		Party of 5 Officers & 80 O.R. sent to man the trenches at MAUREPAS.	
			Brigade moved to GROVETOWN near BRAY	
	25th		Brigade moved to MERICOURT L'ABBE	
	26th		Brigade moved to WARLOY	
	27th		Brigade moved to TEUTONCOURT.	
	28th		At rest in camp at TEUTONCOURT.	
	29th		— — — —	
	30th		— — — —	
	31st		— — — —	

9th TRENCH MORTAR BRIGADE. No. .... Date ....

W. Taylor Capt R.F.A.
Comd 9th Div. T.M. Bde

2353 Wt. W2544/1454 700,000 5/15 D. D. & L. A.D.S.S./Forms/C. 2118.

81.

9th Divisional Artillery.

9th DIVISIONAL TRENCH MORTAR BRIGADE

APRIL 1918.

9th T.M's.

Instructions regarding War Diaries and Intelligence Summaries are contained in F. S. Regs., Part II. and the Staff Manual respectively. Title pages will be prepared in manuscript.

WAR DIARY
or
~~INTELLIGENCE SUMMARY~~.
(Erase heading not required.)

Army Form C. 2118.

Vol 22

Place	Date	Hour	Summary of Events and Information	Remarks and references to Appendices
TEUTENCOURT	1st April		Brigade moved to BOURDON	
	2nd ..		Resting at BOURDON	
	3rd ..		Brigade entrained at Hangest for camp at Daylight Corner near KEMMEL	
NEAR KEMMEL	4th ..		Relieved 1st Australian T.M. Bde in the line taking over 6 6" NEWTON T M's in the line & handing over 6 in exchange.	
	5th ..		Personnel engaged in putting gun positions in order.	
	6th ..		6 6" NEWTON T M's received from 2nd Army School taken up the line & put into gun positions. DTMO moved to Advanced Hdqrs at SPOIL BANK	
	7th ..		Personnel engaged on gun positions	
	8th ..		6 6" NEWTON T M's in the line handed over to 19th Divn T.M. Bde & 6 received in exchange	
	9th ..		1 round fired registration	
	10th ..		6 rounds fired retaliation	
	11th ..		50 rounds fired at Infantry's request retaliation with good effect. 6 6" NEWTON T M's received from 19th T.M. Bde sent to DADOS	
	12th ..		12 rounds fired retaliation	
	13th ..		16	

2353 Wt. W2544/1454 700,000 5/15 D. D. & L. A.D.S.S./Forms/C. 2118.

Instructions regarding War Diaries and Intelligence Summaries are contained in F. S. Regs., Part II. and the Staff Manual respectively. Title pages will be prepared in manuscript.

WAR DIARY
~~or~~
~~INTELLIGENCE SUMMARY.~~
(Erase heading not required.)

Army Form C. 2118.

Place	Date	Hour	Summary of Events and Information	Remarks and references to Appendices
NEAR KEMMEL	14th April		10 rounds fired registration of guns from new emplacements.	
	15th ..		Orders received from D.A. to remove all guns from the line. This was successfully carried out during the night of 15th + 16th.	
ARAGON CAMP	16th ..		Brigade with the D.A.C. at ARAGON CAMP	
	17th ..		Brigade moved to camp near BOESCHEPE. 3 Officers + 59 O.R. sent to 9th DAC.	
	18th ..		In camp.	
	19th ..		Brigade moved to camp near POPERINGHE. 20 O.R. sent to ROBSON'S DUMP for work	
NEAR POPERINGHE	20th ..		In camp	
	21st ..		-- --	
	22nd ..		1 6" NEWTON taken up the line + put in position	
	23rd ..		1 6" -- -- -- -- -- -- -- -- Detachment from X/9 under 2nd/Lt. T. R. SCOTT (M.M.) R.F.A. consisting of 1 Sgt. + 7 O.R. went up the line to man the 2 guns in position	
	24th ..		Enemy bombardment. 2nd/Lt T. R. Scott + his detachment reported missing. 2 6" NEWTONS probably lost.	
	25th ..		Moved to new camp near POPERINGHE L 16 b ~~Sheet~~ 27. Lt. R. Wylie R.F.A. + 28 O.R. attached to D/51st Bde R.F.A.	
	26th ..		In camp.	

2353 Wt. W2544/1454 700,000 5/15 D. D. & L. A.D.S.S./Forms/C. 2118.

Instructions regarding War Diaries and Intelligence Summaries are contained in F. S. Regs., Part II. and the Staff Manual respectively. Title pages will be prepared in manuscript.

WAR DIARY

~~or~~

~~INTELLIGENCE SUMMARY.~~

(*Erase heading not required.*)

Army Form C. 2118.

Place	Date	Hour	Summary of Events and Information	Remarks and references to Appendices
NEAR POPERINGHE	27th	April	Personnel engaged on work at dump for 9th D.A.C.	
	28th	- -		
	29th	- -		
	30th	- -		

9th TRENCH MORTAR BRIGADE

1/5/18. Date

H. L. Taylor Capt. R.F.A.
Comd'g 9th Div T. M. Bde

2353 Wt. W2544/1454 700,000 5/15 D. D. & L. A.D.S.S./Forms/C. 2118.

9. T.M. BDE

Instructions regarding War Diaries and Intelligence Summaries are contained in F. S. Regs., Part II. and the Staff Manual respectively. Title pages will be prepared in manuscript.

WAR DIARY
or
INTELLIGENCE SUMMARY.
(Erase heading not required.)

Army Form C. 2[illegible]8.

VR 23

Place	Date	Hour	Summary of Events and Information	Remarks and references to Appendices
CAMP NEAR POPERINGHE	May 1st to 12th		During this period personnel were employed on work at Dump for D.A.C. [illegible] Officer & 28 O.R. were also attached to II/51st Bde R.F.A.	
	May 13th		Brigade moved to new camp near WINNIZEELE	
	14th to 16th		In camp	
CAMP NEAR RACQUINGHEM	17th		Brigade moved to camp near RACQUINGHEM Map ref. A 10 a 3.5 Sheet 36A	
	18th		[illegible] from [illegible] During the night of 18th/19th the camp was bombed	
	19th		by enemy aircraft 2 men (Gnr Orme & Gnr Harris) being wounded. No material damage was done.	
	20th		Draft of 10 O.R. posted to this unit from Base details.	
	21st to 25th		Brigade at rest. Personnel engaged in Gun Drill & new draft instructed in T.M. work. Box Respirators were inspected by Div. Gas N.C.O. on 23rd	
THIEUSHOUK	26th		Brigade moved by Motor Lorries to THIEUSHOUK Map ref. Q 35 & 30 20. & relieved 30th Divn T.M. Bde in the line taking over 3 6" NEWTON T.Ms & handing 3 in exchange. Detachment from Y/9 under 2/Lt C. [illegible] Kennedy RFA went up to the line to man guns.	
	27th		Gun emplacements being put in order & wires laid etc.	

2353 Wt W2544/1454 700,000 5/15 D. D. & L. A.D.S.S./Forms/C. 2118.

86

Instructions regarding War Diaries and Intelligence Summaries are contained in F. S. Regs., Part II. and the Staff Manual respectively. Title pages will be prepared in manuscript.

WAR DIARY

or

~~INTELLIGENCE SUMMARY.~~

(Erase heading not required.)

Army Form C. 2118.

Place	Date	Hour	Summary of Events and Information	Remarks and references to Appendices
HIEUSHOCK	May 28th		Hdqrs + personnel not in the line moved to camp near STEENVOORDE Map ref. G 14.c central.	
			Fired 10 rounds at night on Poiwey + X roads in enemy lines with good effect	
	" 29th		Fired 8 rounds registration. About 10 P.M. enemy air-craft dropped bombs on the mens billet near the line, setting fire to same + destroying component parts of the Ammunition. Mens kits were also destroyed, fortunately personnel escaped injury	
	" 30th		Work continued on gun emplacements	
	" 31st		— — —	

9TH TRENCH MORTAR BRIGADE. ....No. 31/5/18 Date.

H. Taylor Capt. R.F.A.
D.T.M.O. 9th Div.

8

9. T.M. Bde.

Instructions regarding War Diaries and Intelligence Summaries are contained in F. S. Regs., Part II. and the Staff Manual respectively. Title pages will be prepared in manuscript.

WAR DIARY
or
INTELLIGENCE SUMMARY.
(Erase heading not required.)

Army Form C. 2118.

VR 24

Place	Date	Hour	Summary of Events and Information	Remarks and references to Appendices
NEAR THIEUSHOUK	June 1st		Personnel engaged on gun emplacements.	
	2nd		Hdqrs moved to farmhouse near CAESTRE Q 33. d 75. 90 Sheet 27 S.E.	
NEAR CAESTRE	3rd		Y/9 fired 119 rounds, 25 in day time & 94 at night bombarding METERUN as per Operation Order. Bombardment successful.	
	4th		Y/9 fired 40 rounds into METERUN with good effect, General [illegible] watching the Mortars in action. X/9 were at work on new gun emplacements.	
	5th		Y/9 fired 10 rounds. Work continued on new positions. Lieut. J. F. Jones [illegible] & 2 O.R. proceeded to 2nd Army T.M. School for course.	
	6th		Y/9 fired 66 rounds into METERUN at request of Infantry to assist them in night operations.	
	7th		Y/9 fired 33 rounds with good effect.	
	8th		Y/9 fired 68 rounds & obtained good results.	
	9th		Y/9 fired 31 rounds 6 being registration of new gun.	
	10th		Y/9 fired 89 rounds 48 of which were a barrage in support of infantry [illegible]	
	11th		Y/9 fired 3[illegible] rounds direct hits were observed on enemy [illegible]	
	12th		Y/9 fired 73 rounds with good results & [illegible] to [illegible] a very night [illegible]	

88

Instructions regarding War Diaries and Intelligence Summaries are contained in F. S. Regs., Part II. and the Staff Manual respectively. Title pages will be prepared in manuscript.

WAR DIARY
or
~~INTELLIGENCE SUMMARY.~~
(Erase heading not required.)

Army Form C. 2118.

Place	Date	Hour	Summary of Events and Information	Remarks and references to Appendices
NEAR CAESTRE	June 13th		Y/9 fired 55 rounds but results were poor owing to a high wind.	
	" 14th		Y/9 fired 96 rounds & good results were obtained.	
	" 15th		Y/9 fired 154 rounds, barrage in support of Infantry raid. Also fired 73 rounds in addition with good results.	
	" 16th		Y/9 fired 71 rounds good results obtained.	
	" 17th		Y/9 fired 41 rounds effective results.	
	" 18th		Capt. J. MacMurray R.F.A. rejoined the unit & took over the Command of the Brigade vice Capt H. W. Taylor. Y/9 fired 96 rounds with good results a house being set on fire	
	" 19th		Y/9 fired 143 rounds offensive & barrage for Infantry raid.	
	" 20th		Work on new emplacements.	
	" 21st		Y/9 fired 76 rounds several direct hits were observed on a house which was demolished.	
	" 22nd		Work continued on new emplacements.	
	" 23rd		X/9 fired 76 rounds, registration & barrage in support of Infantry attack good results.	
	" 24th		2/Lieut. K. C. Boast. R.F.A. & 9 O.R. proceeded to 2nd Army T.M. School for course. Work continued on new emplacements.	
	" 25th		Y/9 fired 86 rounds on enemy trenches with good effect.	

89

2353 Wt. W2541/1454 700,000 5/15 D. D. & L. A.D.S.S./Forms/C. 2118.

Instructions regarding War Diaries and Intelligence Summaries are contained in F. S. Regs., Part II. and the Staff Manual respectively. Title pages will be prepared in manuscript.

WAR DIARY

or

~~INTELLIGENCE~~ SUMMARY.

(Erase heading not required.)

Army Form C. 2118.

Place	Date	Hour	Summary of Events and Information	Remarks and references to Appendices
NEAR CAESTRE.	June 26th		Y/9 fired 80 rounds. 4 direct hits were observed, & front of a large building demolished.	
	" 27th		Y/9 fired 120 rounds on enemy trenches good results were obtained	
	" 28th		Y/9 fired 36 rounds on enemy trenches & wire effective results.	
	" 29th		Y/9 fired 126 rounds on enemy trench. 5 direct hits observed on enemy M.G. post.	
	" 30th		Y/9 fired 208 rounds completely demolishing houses & making gaps in hedge.	

[illegible signature]
Capt. R.F.A.
Comd'g 9th Div. T.M. Brigade.

9TH TRENCH MORTAR BRIGADE.
No. ....
Date. 1/7/17

90

2353 Wt. W2544/1454 700,000 5/15 D. D. & L. A.D.S.S./Forms/C. 2118.

Army Form C. 2118.

WAR DIARY
~~or~~
~~INTELLIGENCE SUMMARY.~~

(Erase heading not required.)

Instructions regarding War Diaries and Intelligence Summaries are contained in F. S. Regs., Part II. and the Staff Manual respectively. Title pages will be prepared in manuscript.

Place	Date	Hour	Summary of Events and Information	Remarks and references to Appendices
NEAR CAESTRE Q33 a 75. 90 Sheet 27 S.E.	1st July		Battery positions in the line were heavily shelled at 9 AM. Capt W Price Jones RFA O.C. X/9 wounded, & admitted to Hospital. 2/Lieut G. F. Charnley RFA Y/9 slightly wounded remained at duty. X/9 fired 50 rounds on houses in METEREN with good effect.	
	2nd		X/9 fired 122 rounds to demolish houses in METEREN, good results were obtained	
	3rd		X/9 fired 105 rounds demolishing walls & houses in METEREN.	
	4th		X/9 fired 138 rounds on houses in METEREN with good effect. Draft from Base consisting of 1 Cpl 1 Bdr & 9 Gnrs joined Brigade.	
	5th		X/9 fired 54 rounds on enemy trench. good results.	
	6th		X/9 fired 122 rounds on selected targets in METEREN as per 9th D.A. Operation Order No 237. Artillery bombardment to destroy enemy defences.	
	7th		X/9 fired 113 rounds on suspected enemy T.M. emplacement, & houses in METEREN, several direct hits obtained	
	8th		X/9 fired 62 rounds on houses & trench in METEREN several direct hits were observed	
	9th		X/9 fired 124 rounds on Brewery, houses & cross-roads in METEREN good results obtained	
	10th		X/9 fired 134 rounds on sniper's post, houses & trench in METEREN. Houses much damaged & hedge in front of trench blown up.	

9. T.M. Bde.

Instructions regarding War Diaries and Intelligence Summaries are contained in F. S. Regs., Part II. and the Staff Manual respectively. Title pages will be prepared in manuscript.

WAR DIARY
or
~~INTELLIGENCE SUMMARY.~~
(Erase heading not required.)

Army Form C. 2118.

Vol 25

Place	Date	Hour	Summary of Events and Information	Remarks and references to Appendices
NEAR CAESTRE Q33 d 75. 90 Sheet 27 S.E.	11th July		X/9 fired 70 rounds on METEREN. Houses damaged + direct hits observed on Cross Roads.	
	12th "		X/9 fired 59 rounds to assist Infantry during raid, + also at enemy T.M. Prisoner captured by Infantry stated our T.M.'s had caused severe casualties to enemy.	
	13th "		X/9 fired 81 rounds on houses in METEREN + enemy trenches with good results.	
	14th "		X/9 fired 122 rounds on enemy M.G. post, trench + houses in METEREN. good effect.	
	15th "		No firing took place owing to adverse weather conditions.	
	16th "		X/9 fired 40 rounds on enemy M.G. post + hostile T.M. with good effect. 6 Signallers posted to Brigade from D.A.C.	
	17th "		X/9 fired 100 rounds on Brewery + houses in METEREN. numerous direct hits observed.	
	18th "		X/9 fired 32 rounds damaging houses in METEREN.	
	19th "		X/9 fired 107 rounds as per 9th D.A. Operation Order No 239. artillery bombardment previous to the attack on METEREN, which was successfully undertaken.	
	20th " to 31st		10 O.R. sent to 2nd Army T.M. School for course. No firing took place during this period. Personnel engaged removing guns from old positions having been put out of range after recent operations. Also engaged making dug outs + digging trench in connection with same. Light Minnenwerfers (2 complete) were salved, also amn for same	

78

Army Form C. 2118.

Instructions regarding War Diaries and Intelligence Summaries are contained in F. S. Regs., Part II. and the Staff Manual respectively. Title pages will be prepared in manuscript.

WAR DIARY
~~or~~
~~INTELLIGENCE SUMMARY.~~
(Erase heading not required.)

Place	Date	Hour	Summary of Events and Information	Remarks and references to Appendices
NEAR CAESTRE Q33 d.75.90	26th July		Draft from Base consisting of 1 Cpl 1 Bdr & 5 Gnrs joined the Brigade.	
Sheet 27 S.E.	30th "		Enemy shell landed in trench near mens dug-out killing 2 Gunners & wounding 1 Bdr.	

9TH TRENCH MORTAR BRIGADE.
.... No.
31/7/1918 Date.

[signature]
Capt. R.F.A.
Comd'g 9th Div T.M. Brigade.

2353 Wt. W2544/1454 700,000 5/15 D. D. & L. A.D.S.S./Forms/C. 2118.

8

9th T.M. BDE

WAR DIARY
or
INTELLIGENCE SUMMARY.
(Erase heading not required.)

Army Form C. 2118.

Vol 26

76

Instructions regarding War Diaries and Intelligence Summaries are contained in F. S. Regs., Part II. and the Staff Manual respectively. Title pages will be prepared in manuscript.

Place	Date	Hour	Summary of Events and Information	Remarks and references to Appendices
NEAR CAESTRE Q.32.d.75.90 Sheet 27 S.E.	1st Aug to 15th		During this period the Brigade was engaged constructing new gun emplacements putting guns into position & work on Officers & mens dugouts also making tracks leading to same. On the 10th inst 1 Officer & 10 O.R. proceeded to 2nd Army T.M. School for course on T.Ms.	
	16th Aug		46 rounds were fired principally registration from new positions	
	17th		A further 4 rounds were fired registration	
	18th		23 rounds were fired [illegible] artillery bombardment as per Operation Order No 248 [illegible] the infantry attack [illegible] which was successful	
	19th to 22nd		No firing took place during this period	
	22nd		36 rounds were fired on suspected Machine Gun posts, with good results	
	23rd		No firing took place	
	24th		12 rounds were fired registration	
	25th to 27th		No firing took place during this period	
	28th		27 rounds were fired on suspected Machine Gun posts.	

2353 Wt W2544/1454 700,000 5/15 D. D. & L. A.D.S.S./Forms/C. 2118.

Army Form C. 2118.

WAR DIARY

or

INTELLIGENCE SUMMARY

(*Erase heading not required.*)

Instructions regarding War Diaries and Intelligence Summaries are contained in F. S. Regs., Part I. and the Staff Manual respectively. Title pages will be prepared in manuscript.

Place	Date	Hour	Summary of Events and Information	Remarks and references to Appendices
NEAR CAESTRE	29th Aug		45 rounds were fired on suspected Machine Gun posts	
Q23 d 75. 90	30th		No firing took place.	
Sheet 27 S.E.	31st		T.Ms & ammunition being collected owing to enemy withdrawl	

9TH TRENCH MORTAR BRIGADE.
..................No.
31/8/1918 Date.

[signature]
Capt R.F.A.
Comdg 9th Div T.M. Brigade

77

Instructions regarding War Diaries and Intelligence Summaries are contained in F. S. Regs., Part II. and the Staff Manual respectively. Title pages will be prepared in manuscript.

WAR DIARY
or
INTELLIGENCE SUMMARY.
(Erase heading not required.)

Army Form C. 2118.

9 D T M Bty

Vol 27

Place	Date	Hour	Summary of Events and Information	Remarks and references to Appendices
NEAR CAESTRE Q33 a 75.90 Sheet 27	1st Sept to 8th		Personnel engaged in salving 6" T.M. ammunition, sending same to A.R.P. All guns, beds etc brought down from the line, cleaned up & overhauled.	
	9th		At Rest	
	10th		1 Officer & 20 O.R. proceeded to Dump near BALLIEUL for salvage work. 20 O.R. also sent in G.S. Wagons from B.A.C. to forward areas for salvage work.	
	11th		Party sent to forward areas for salvage as on the 10th inst	
	12th		Brigade moved by Lorries to camp near HOUTKERQUE. Map ref. E10. a 40.30 Sheet 27	
NEAR HOUTKERQUE	13th & 14th		At Rest.	
	15th		Capt C.A. Lewis R.F.A. Lt. C.A.R. Kennedy R.F.A. & 68 O.R. proceeded to Dump for work in connection with 9th D.A.	
	16th to 23rd		At Rest	
	24th		Brigade moved by Lorries to Camp near PROVEN. Map ref. F28 c 8.5 Sheet 27.	
	25th		Capt C.A. Lewis, Lt. C.A.R. Kennedy & personnel returned to unit from dump leaving 11 O.R. at same.	
	21st		At Rest	
	27th		Personnel moved to forward area near YPRES	

2353 Wt W2544/1454 700,000 5/15 D. D. & L. A.D.S.S./Forms/C. 2118.

Instructions regarding War Diaries and Intelligence Summaries are contained in F. S. Regs., Part II. and the Staff Manual respectively. Title pages will be prepared in manuscript.

WAR DIARY
or
INTELLIGENCE SUMMARY.
(Erase heading not required.)

Army Form C. 2118.

Place	Date	Hour	Summary of Events and Information	Remarks and references to Appendices
YPRES.	Sept 28th		25 OR sent to A.R.P Remainder of Brigade engaged in manning 4.2. H.V. guns which were captured during the morning.	
			1 OR wounded	
	29th		Brigade moved to New Camp situated between YPRES and POTIJZE (I 9. a 1. 8)	
			10 OR sent to 2nd Army Trench Mortar School	
	30th		Move to new camp completed	

J MacMurray
CAPT. R.F.A.
COMD'G 9th DIV. T.M.B.

2353 Wt. W2544/1454 700,000 5/15 D. D. & L. A.D.S.S./Forms/C. 2118.

Instructions regarding War Diaries and Intelligence Summaries are contained in F. S. Regs., Part II. and the Staff Manual respectively. Title pages will be prepared in manuscript.

WAR DIARY
or
~~INTELLIGENCE~~ SUMMARY.
(Erase heading not required.)

Army Form C. 2118.

T M Btys
Vol. 28

Place	Date	Hour	Summary of Events and Information	Remarks and references to Appendices
	Oct			
POTIJZE	1st		In camp at I9a.1.8. (Sheet 28)	
	2nd-3rd		In camp at I9a1.8. (Sheet 28).	
KEYBERG	4th		Brigade moved to new camp near Keyberg E20.c.50.10 (28)	
	5th		Completed the move to camp at Keyberg. Officer and men working at ARP rejoined the unit	
LEDEGHEM	6th		8 Guns put in action in area L2.c.7.7 (Sheet 28) Forward HQ and billets established at F1.a.6.2 (28).	
	7th		Ammunition taken up to the new gun positions. Work carried out on gun-pits. Remainder of Brigade engaged on work in new camp near Keyberg	
	8th		2nd Lieut H.P. Gerrard and 8 O.R. sent forward to complete work on gun pits	
	9th to 11th		Work continued on the gun emplacements. Ammunition carried. 2 Medium Minnenwerfers salvaged near Keyberg	
	12th		Work continued on gun emplacements. Remainder of stores moved from camp near POTIJZE to camp near KEYBERG. 2. O.R's wounded.	
	13th		Work completed on gun emplacements. Men in camp near KEYBERG.	

2353 Wt W2544/1454 700,000 5/15 D. D. & L. A.D.S.S./Forms/C. 2118.

Instructions regarding War Diaries and Intelligence Summaries are contained in F. S. Regs., Part II. and the Staff Manual respectively. Title pages will be prepared in manuscript.

WAR DIARY

~~or~~

~~INTELLIGENCE SUMMARY.~~

(Erase heading not required.)

Army Form C. 2118.

Place	Date	Hour	Summary of Events and Information	Remarks and references to Appendices
	Oct.			
	13th		2. Special beds and carriages were received from 4 Mobile workshops. On the night of the 13th the guns and teams were placed in a farm near the front line	
	14th		In support of the attack on the Ledghem front 8 standing mortars were in action 140 Rds were fired for the barrage. At Zero hour the Officer i/c of the Mobile Mortars acting on instructions from G.O.C. Infantry Brigade carrying out the attack proceeded to engage an enemy pillbox containing MG's which were checking the advance. The pillbox however was taken before the guns got into action. 2½ hours after the attack commenced the enemy barrage had slackened sufficiently to enable an advance to be made with reasonable safety. On gaining touch with the Infantry it was found they were checked by the farm at L5.b.3.9 in which were several MG's and 77 mm gun firing on ROLLIGHEM CAPELLE. The mortars were brought into action behind a farmhouse within 700x of the enemy 40 Rds	

Instructions regarding War Diaries and Intelligence Summaries are contained in F. S. Regs., Part II. and the Staff Manual respectively. Title pages will be prepared in manuscript.

WAR DIARY

~~or~~

~~INTELLIGENCE SUMMARY.~~

(*Erase heading not required.*)

Army Form C. 21

Place	Date	Hour	Summary of Events and Information	Remarks and references to Appendices
	Oct cont 14th		were fired at the MG's and gun The detachment of the latter were killed or wounded and the MG's were silenced thus enabling the Infantry to advance The mortars closely following up the Infantry next came into action behind a wood at G 3 a (29) but were unable to silence the MG's that were checking the advance owing to the difficulty experienced in locating them.	
	15th		When the attack was renewed the two mobile mortars took part in the barrage firing on suspected MG's. 1. OR. wounded during this operation. Having refilled with ammunition guns then advanced with the infantry meeting little opposition. The 77 mm gun near WINKEL ST ELOI was fired during the barrage. The mobile mortars were brought into action in Guerne the infantry having halted East of LE CHAT Firing from behind GUERNE CHURCH at H 11. a. 1. 6. (Sheet 29) one of the mortars dispersed a party of the enemy who were attempting to dig in on the opposite bank of the Lys Constant fire was maintained throughout the night in order to give the	

2353 Wt W2544/1454 700,000 5/15 D. D. & L. A.D.S.S./Forms/C. 2118.

Instructions regarding War Diaries and Intelligence Summaries are contained in F. S. Regs., Part II. and the Staff Manual respectively. Title pages will be prepared in manuscript.

WAR DIARY
~~or~~
~~INTELLIGENCE~~ SUMMARY.
(*Erase heading not required.*)

Army Form C. 2118.

Place	Date	Hour	Summary of Events and Information	Remarks and references to Appendices
	Oct			
	15th		enemy no opportunity of digging in. Rations and ammunition were obtained by means of a German motor lorry. On the 15th however	
WINKEL ST ELOI			this was put out of working order by a machine gun bullet HQ moved to WINKEL ST ELOI	
	16th		On the afternoon of the 16th the other mortar was put in at H 4. d 7.5 to fire on a light minnenwerfer which fired from the vicinity of HARLEBEKE church. This was silenced. During the three days operations a total of 470 Rounds were fired	
	17th		Enemy bombarded CUERNE. 1. Off and 5 OR wounded. In the afternoon the two mobile mortars were fired. One at a field gun reported just over the bridge in HARLEBEKE at H 11. b. 6.3 The mortar at the church fired at MG's and was withdrawn as the enemy shelled the area heavily. This gun was eventually put out of action by a 5.9" shell	
	18th		Mortars were moved to Hulste B 22. a 0.6. (29)	
	19th		No firing	

Instructions regarding War Diaries and Intelligence Summaries are contained in F. S. Regs., Part II. and the Staff Manual respectively. Title pages will be prepared in manuscript.

WAR DIARY
or
INTELLIGENCE SUMMARY.
(*Erase heading not required.*)

Army Form C. 2118.

Place	Date	Hour	Summary of Events and Information	Remarks and references to Appendices
	Oct 20th		Mobile mortars again followed up the infantry but their assistance was not required	
	21st		No attack. Detachments on the mortars were relieved. Forward	
HULSTE			HQ moved to BEVEREN. C 25 d. 4.5 (29) Rear HQ moved to HULSTE. B22 a. 0.6 (29)	
	22nd		Attack renewed Mortars sent forward 2 hours after Zero hour but owing to mud and enemy MG's. behind our line were unable to get into ~~at~~ touch with the infantry	
	23rd		Two more beds and, carriages of a later type drawn from Ordinance	
	24th		In billets 2 Mortars prepared for action Ammunition dumped at Belgick X Roads. I 17 c 7. 2 Sheet 29	
	25th		Attack continued 1 Gun fired on enemy MG's at Zero hour. Mortars	
BEVEREN			advanced 1½ hours after Zero. and fired on point P2. d 9. 0 where the infantry had been checked. The MG's were silenced and the infantry enabled to advance Rear. HQ moved to BEVEREN. C 25 d 4.5	

Instructions regarding War Diaries and Intelligence Summaries are contained in F. S. Regs., Part II. and the Staff Manual respectively. Title pages will be prepared in manuscript.

WAR DIARY

~~or~~

~~INTELLIGENCE~~ SUMMARY.

(Erase heading not required.)

Army Form C. 2118.

Place	Date	Hour	Summary of Events and Information	Remarks and references to Appendices
	Oct			
	25th		During this attack the unit also fired 3 77mm guns in the barrage	
	26th		No firing owing to clear weather and exposed nature of surrounding country	
	27th		All detachments relieved from the line	
	28th		Brigade at BEVEREN	
	29th		Brigade moved to rest at CUERNE H 10. a 50.30	
CUERNE.	30th		At rest in CUERNE	
	31st		" " CUERNE	

9TH TRENCH MORTAR BRIGADE.
.... No.
31/10/18. Date.

[signature] CAPT. R.F.A.
COMD'G 9TH DIV. T.M.B.

2353 Wt. W2544/1454 700,000 5/15 D. D. & L. A.D.S.S./Forms/C. 2118.

Instructions regarding War Diaries and Intelligence Summaries are contained in F. S. Regs., Part II. and the Staff Manual respectively. Title pages will be prepared in manuscript.

WAR DIARY
or
INTELLIGENCE SUMMARY.
(Erase heading not required.)

Army Form C. 2118.

9th TRENCH MORTAR BDE. 30/11/18.

Place	Date	Hour	Summary of Events and Information	Remarks and references to Appendices
	Nov 1918			
CUERNE	1 - 13		Brigade in billets at CUERNE.	
	14		... moved to VICHTE	
	15		... ... RENAIX	
	16 - 18		... remained in billets at RENAIX	
	19		... moved to NEDERBRAKEL.	
	20		... in billets at NEDERBRAKEL	
	21st		... moved to HOEVE near GOYCK.	
	22nd		... in billets HOEVE.	
	23rd		... moved to TOURNEPPE	
	24th		... in billets at TOURNEPPE	
	25th		... moved to WAVRE.	
	26		... in billets at WAVRE.	
	27		... moved to HUPPAYE.	
	28th		... ... MOXHE	
	29th		... ... AMPSIN	
	30.		... in billets at AMPSIN	

J. MacMurray CAPT. R.F.A.
COMD'G 9TH DIV. T.M.B.

2353 Wt. W2544/1454 700,000 5/15 D. D. & L. A.D.S.S./Forms/C. 2118.

Instructions regarding War Diaries and Intelligence Summaries are contained in F. S. Regs., Part II. and the Staff Manual respectively. Title pages will be prepared in manuscript.

WAR DIARY

~~INTELLIGENCE SUMMARY.~~

(*Erase heading not required.*)

9TH TRENCH MORTAR BRIGADE. No. 31/12/18. Date.

Army Form C. 2118.

Place	Date	Hour	Summary of Events and Information	Remarks and references to Appendices
AMPSIN				
BELGIUM.	1st Dec	1918.	Brigade moved to CHÊNÉE near LIEGE.	
	2 - 3rd		Resting at CHÊNÉE.	
	4		Brigade moved to VERVIERS.	
	5		-- -- -- EUPEN. GERMANY.	
	6		-- -- -- KORNELIMÜNSTER.	
	7		-- -- -- DHORN.	
	8		-- -- -- BERGERHAUSEN.	
	9		-- -- -- BOCKLEMUNDE. near COLOGNE.	
	10 - 12		Resting at BOCKLEMUNDE.	
	13		Brigade marched through COLOGNE, across the RHINE to STAMHIEM.	
	14 - 15		Resting at STAMHIEM.	
	15		Brigade moved to LANGEFEILD.	
	16 - 20		Resting at LANGEFEILD.	
	21		Brigade moved to permanent billets at LÖHDORF near OHLIGS.	
	22 - 31		Personnel engaged in Military & Recreational Training.	

VR 30

H. L. Taylor CAPT. R.E.(?) COMD'G 9TH DIV. T.M.(?)

2353 Wt. W25-1/1454 700,000 5/15 D. D. & L. A.D.S.S./Forms/C. 2118.

9th T.M. Bde.

Instructions regarding War Diaries and Intelligence Summaries are contained in F. S. Regs., Part II. and the Staff Manual respectively. Title pages will be prepared in manuscript.

WAR DIARY

or

~~INTELLIGENCE SUMMARY.~~

(Erase heading not required.)

Army Form C. 2118.

TRENCH MORTAR BRIGADE.

4R 31

Place	Date	Hour	Summary of Events and Information	Remarks and references to Appendices
LOHDORF NEAR OHLIGS. GERMANY.	1st Jan to 31st		During the month personnel of the unit have undergone training with the 6" Mobile Newton T. M. A Sgt Instructor 8th Royal Highlanders, 26th Infy Bde has been attached to the unit, for the purpose of giving instruction in rifle practice, Infantry squad drill, etc. A rifle range has been fitted up, + the personnel have undergone firing practice, good progress being made. 40 N.C.O's + men have been sent to Field Battery's for instruction in horsemanship + stable management, + have not yet completed their training. Fair progress has been made with Education, classes having been formed for German + French, under tuition from Capt. J. Mac Murray. M.C. R.F.A. + Capt. C. A. Lewis. M.C. R.F.A. respectively. A football team has been organised + entered for the Divisional Artillery Cup, also the Divisional Cup. Advantage has also been taken of the gymnasium in the village, for men to undergo gymnastic training + instruction in boxing. Several lectures have been given on demobilization, recruiting for Post Bellum army, + Venereal Disease.	

J MacMurray
CAPT. R.F.A.
COMD'G 9th DIV. T.M.B.

2353 Wt W2544/1454 700,000 5/15 D. D. & L. A.D.S.S./Forms/C. 2118.

www.ingramcontent.com/pod-product-compliance
Lightning Source LLC
Chambersburg PA
CBHW080851230426
43662CB00013B/2070